If My Soul Be Lost

A SELF PORTRAIT

Nandi S. Crosby, Ph.D.

BookSurge Publishing, Charleston, SC

ISBN: 0-7199-5915-2

To order additional copies, please go to
www.Amazon.com

or contact the author:
Dr_WarriorWoman@hotmail.com

Department of Sociology
CSU, Chico
Chico, CA 95929-0445

For my baby brother, Munch
1978-2004

Like Winnie Mandela said,
"A part of my soul went with him...."

ACKNOWLEDGMENTS

Thank you, Mother/Father/God. For *everything*! I especially want to thank you for my baby brother who now sits at your feet.

I must thank Debbi, my new friend in Oklahoma. It's because she asked why this book was not written that I wrote it.

I want to thank my parents for realizing that their story is mine too. Much love.

After listening to me read, "A Million Miles from Vegas," my dearest friend Akinyele told me this was an important book to complete. I finished it because he believed I was the one who should be writing it.

Then there's my Auntie Shelia and Aunt Linda. Although I did not mention their names in the book, they are part of the reason I am the woman I am. They are awesome role models!

Laurie and Tony, my friends and colleagues, were the first to read a draft of this book. Their feedback was pivotal in my willingness to take this from a first to a final draft.

Although I pushed my girl Aprille away during the construction of this book, I felt the entire time she still believed in me. The struggles she's endured to become a stronger Black woman are part of why I was so candid in my own story.

I appreciate J's tell it like it is approach to reviewing this book. If he said it worked, I kept it. If he said it didn't, I tossed it—for the most part.

Of course, I cannot forget to say thank you to my students at CSU, Chico and the women incarcerated at the Leo Chesney Center who tolerated listening to me talk about this book well before the kinks were out.

CONTENTS

$\mathcal{P}$ROLOGUE

Clarifying what I mean when I say I have always felt I would be incarcerated a is difficult task. I don't dabble in metaphor; quite literally, I have felt since the age of ten that I'm going to be incarcerated someday. Perhaps in another life, my mother gave birth to me in a correctional facility. Perhaps the Spirit who guides my life is the same One who overlooks the incarcerated masses and knows better than I do where I am supposed to be.

In the 1970's, while still in elementary school, I often stayed up late to watch the television serial, *Prisoner: Cell Block H.* Having recently purchased the DVD, I see now how campy it was and have to wonder how I was so strongly drawn to it. Nevertheless, at ten years old, I was wrapped so profoundly in the story that I imagined myself fitting there, within the complicity of gang leaders, as an officer's lover or warden's nemesis, and sometimes as a mentor to new recruits. I would be imprisoned, although wrongly accused, because I could never imagine getting into too much trouble. Other inmates would know me as a politicized or political prisoner (terms I learned much later) and employ me to address the administration as their fearless leader. Strangely, though, I never saw myself as an inmate in a woman's prison. Perhaps because of the other mass media I ingested, as documentaries, Hollywood films, radio talk shows, books, and news stories, I saw myself surrounded by male inmates. My ruminations were rooted heavily in what I thought to be the struggles and politics of male prison culture and I seemed to fit there.

I have since, at various times in my adult life, been engaged with prison communities: working as an officer in a maximum security prison for men; falling romantically for inmates; volunteering to help those imprisoned transition into the free world; lecturing on sex and violence issues; joining organized protests against the prison industrial complex; and working diligently as a researcher of sociological phenomena that are uniquely prison constructed. But this self-portrait is not at all about being physically incarcerated. It is an examination of the many dark places I have allowed my intuition, curiosities, and feminist philosophy to take me. It is a journey, mostly, toward healing and liberation.

Although most of my conversations are with college students and professors, most of my fulfillment comes from working with prisoners. Talking to such marginalized, motivated groups makes me feel like I belong somewhere, as if I'm connected to a community of people who want what I want: empowerment, with an edge of desperation. It has been my willingness to embrace the unknown, inside prisons and inside myself, that moves me, uplifts me, and carries me forward.

THE LEGEND OF JOE EDISION

For more than twenty-two years, my uncle worked as a correctional officer. He recently retired with the status of Major, carrying with him the respect of his peers and the thousands of inmates whose lives he touched. Early in his tenure, he spent countless hours addressing my curiosities about what inmates wore, what they ate, things they said. For example, in Maryland where we lived, prisoners wear their own clothes. Inmates in movies wear state-issued, striped or bland, unattractive uniforms. Thus, I found it fascinating that on any given day, prisoners walked the grounds of Maryland's penitentiaries adorned in name-brand jeans, velour sweat suits, and mattress-pressed collar shirts. I was equally enthralled by my uncle's lessons of prison lingo, assaults, and the administration's response to sex between inmates. I was satisfied with knowing the basics—when I was a teenager.

My inquires grew more complex, my curiosities more deep, when I became an adult. My uncle had recently accepted a job as Captain at the Maryland House of Corrections, Annex, a brand-new maximum-security prison for men. His rise through the ranks was swift and his ability to separate the politics of his personal and professional lives was flawless. He had also learned extremely well how to exercise the first rule of thumb taught to him many years prior: be fair, firm, and impartial in all matters concerning prisoners.

During my first year out of college, I applied for a career as a correctional officer, being so inspired by my uncle's ability to do well. I expressed a desire to work in a minimum-security facility, though, thinking that to do so would give me the insight I wanted and a relative assurance of safety. After a year or so of rigorous testing, background checks, and health exams, I received a call from the State asking if I would accept a position — in the same new maximum security facility where my uncle worked. I accepted. I was twenty-two years old then.

Before being allowed to enter the facility, I was required to attend Maryland's standard 5-week training academy. The paramilitary program was a listless educational event that did little to prepare me for what was in store at the Annex. I graduated the academy with honors and showed up to work, proud, with my blue ribbon. On my first day at the prison, a veteran officer remarked that my ribbon was useless for saving my own life, and that I should remove it so as not to appear pretentious to the other officers or "square" to the inmates.

At the time of such early development of the Annex, only two of the nine buildings were opened and prepared to house inmates. Every building is shaped like a cross and holds ninety-six inmates on each of the four wings. In the middle of the building is the control center that houses security equipment such as handcuffs and pepper spray, and acts as the 360-

degree panoptic lens for officers to monitor what happens on each wing. There are two tiers to each wing and two inmates per cell. To be successful as an officer at the Annex, one has to believe that prisoners are less than human. How else could they kill? How else could we justify the work we were doing? Furthermore, we were required to wear shank-proof vests that served a dual function, cognitively. First, it gave one a false sense of security. If an inmate wants to kill an officer in a vest, he will repeatedly stab her or him in the head. Second, its physical heaviness was a constant reminder that threats to one's life were always looming, which is the same as saying that inmates are always about to kill officers.

Joe Edison was housed on C wing of B building. The first time I saw him, about one month after beginning my job there, I was working C wing. Joe Edison was approximately my age. I had never met him, but was aware of stories about him that grew more grand each time I heard them. People on the streets never call him "Joe." We refer to him as Joe Edison, always, much like the way we speak about celebrities as Michael Jackson instead of Mike, or Leonard Peltier instead of Lenny. Joe Edison was a murderer and people in the projects feared him. Joe Edison and I were from the same large project community in Baltimore, and most of my family and friends even today have a story to tell of his legend.

My grandmother said, "He killed the wrong guy at first, and then broke out of jail to get the right guy."

My mother commented, "He killed some people, then he roamed the streets dressed in women's clothes, right up under the police for a long time. He was bad!"

My cousin remarked, "Joe Edison kilt people! A whole bunch o' people! Then he busted out of jail just so he could kill witnesses. He was on the America's Most Wanted list for a long time."

The actual number of people Joe Edison killed was not a pressing issue for me. What was most salient in my mind was how awesome was the legend of Joe Edison, and which fine lines divided us now that I stood just inches from him. Initially, I was mesmerized — mostly by the fact that he stood barely 5'5" and was lean in stature; stories about him could make one think he was eight-feet tall. He was a caramel colored Black man with humble green eyes. With such smooth skin and very little facial hair, I understood how he was successful at staying out of plain view of police by dressing as a woman. When he was on the streets, I had never peered at him through window shades, had never witnessed him harm or terrorize anyone, and certainly, I was committed to being fair, firm, and impartial toward him. Still, I was scared of Joe Edison.

Noticing the fear I had been carrying with me, Uncle told me never to forget *it*, never to let go of the drive to stay alert and on guard. But my fear was complex. It was not just a common fear of being beaten or held captive by inmates like Joe Edison. Nor was it the fear of being raped, as with most female officers in male facilities. My fear was partly linked to my rejection of a sense of entitlement that I had been taught to presume while in the academy: they were criminals (which is supposed to mean they lack values and morals), and I was the leader, the more "righteous" of us two. I knew I had not yet done much to earn respect from prisoners and was clear that they would not give it simply because I showed up. As any correctional officer will tell, inmates have very little respect for the job and any honor given to an officer is earned long and hard. Furthermore, for African American inmates who had learned to internalize even just a little of Afrocentric discourse, I was the *true* enemy of our people. After all, for several dollars per hour, I had committed to assure citizens of the freeworld that I would do all I could to keep inmates from harming them again — including killing these men, most of whom were Black, if they attempted to escape. Inmates, thus, called me a "house nigger," a traitor to my race. In my attempt to reject all the assumptions and accusations that come with being an officer, I had hoped to be given the same opportunities to garner respect, as did Uncle, working for it from the ground up.

What's more, I did not want my gender to be as an issue in my interactions with inmates. Having no say in the matter, they always saw me as female — shifting their voices, their gazes, and their resentment when I entered a wing. I often struggled with sexual power, which mainly stemmed from my unwillingness to employ femininity to get them to do what I wanted. Many female officers in male institutions begin their careers wanting to eschew the power their feminine presence commands. They are conscious about the power implicit in their bodies and work hard to diminish it. This is an uphill battle because, on the one hand, inmates will never let women tuck away the fact that we are women. They remind us at every twist and turn that we are different from them and valued primarily to the degree that we are willing to stay present in our bodies. On the other hand, female officers who are able to resist being seen only as female will necessarily be treated like men, or worse, like lesbians: "women who hate men." In either case, there is no such thing as gender neutrality in prison. Male inmates are always trying to be *men*.

At the Annex, when inmates exit their cells during meals to pick up their trays, officers are supposed to step inside the cell and conduct a general security check including physically inspecting the walls. Once inside the cell, the officer is out of view from the person running the control center; therefore, we had to make sure the inmates would, in fact, leave the cell. Sometimes inmates refused and encouraged officers, namely women, to enter their tiny cells while they were still inside. This is a dangerous test by inmates to see how easily officers will violate security codes. I gave in a handful of times, and thankfully, I never got hurt. And just like failing this test and being intuitively aware of what was wrong with my choice to do so, I was tested many, many times. Sometimes I passed. Other times, I did not.

One afternoon while working the 3-11 p.m. shift on Joe Edison's wing, I lost it. During most of the day, inmates are allowed out of their cells to attend social activities in the day room or to be present on the tier to do laundry. On this day, at least fifty of the ninety-six inmates on C wing were roaming the tiers. This was a sign of poor security. I kept running between the upper and lower tiers asking the inmates to go to their cells or the day room. As one inmate locked in, another came out. They had excuses upon excuses about why they needed to be somewhere other than where they were supposed to be.

One inmate had been demanding that I make a call to request information about his visit to the nurse or with family, I cannot remember which now. He had gotten so annoyed that at one point he stood very close to my face and yelled about how poorly I was doing my job. I asked him to step back and stop yelling. He continued to scream, this time calling me a dyke and saying that I had no business being there in the first place. With such a sizeable captive audience of men, including the piercing green eyes belonging to Joe Edison, and my being near tears from the stress, I called my supervisor on the radio and asked for a break. I was granted the break, but could never get back the respect I lost that day.

See, prison is a place where no one tolerates weakness of any kind. To lose face or show vulnerability means that you are not a "real man," which one is expected to be even if she is a woman. In other words, femininity is confirmation that one deserves no respect for the remainder of their time . Women are expected to deal with being victimized and quiet, even during times when they are "gunned down," the penultimate experience of degradation when an inmate can catch a female officer off guard and masturbate to completion, a surreal experience of violation second only to rape itself.

After twelve months at the Annex, I left to attend graduate school in Atlanta. Joe Edison never spoke one word to me during that year. He was quiet most of the time and did not converse with many people. I imagined myself living like Joe Edison if I were convicted to spend the remainder of my life in prison, but knew I would be different because respect and power always seemed to come from my engaging people, from my use of words.

Joe Edison is still confined to a penitentiary in Maryland. More than fifteen years after I first encountered him, I still wonder about inmates like him, men and women who grow up in the projects creating a whirlwind of fear and fury, and then disappearing into silence. Mostly I wonder what happens to their legends, stories that we tell about people like Joe Edison and the degree to which they stir in ordinary people like me, a desire to look fear and fury in the eye, chase down the tornado, and examine what the journey inside has forced us to become.

$\mathcal{T}$HE GHETTO AIN'T SO BAD

Whenever I talk about the Black community to college students and scholars—of every race—two things tend to happen. First, they speak about poverty, hard times, drugs, and violence as if these capture the essence of contemporary Black America. Second, when I do engage them about poverty and the projects, they resist seeing what's okay about the 'hood. I maintain that "Black" doesn't just mean hard times and the ghetto ain't so bad, although it is definitely not what it used to be.

As a child, I had no analytical skills to categorize my social class. My brother and I qualified for the free breakfast and free lunch programs at school, but then so did everyone around my way. When my mother gave me two one-dollar food stamps to purchase items from Mr. Willie's immobile bus-turned-convenience-store across the street, I did not think those food stamps meant we were poor. I was to buy three eggs to go with Sunday breakfast and six icing-coated cookies for my big brother and me to snack on later. We had no air conditioning so when it was too hot to cook, my mother would prepare tuna from the can, then place it on lettuce with a side of Saltine crackers.

If she were low on mayonnaise, she would equip my brother or me with a small cup and say, "Go ax Miss Mary for some mayonnaise. If she don't ha' none, ax Miss Cynthia."

I'd hike my skinny 6-year-old self next door, holler up at the window or through the mailbox, "Miss Mary, my muvva said, 'do you got a li'l bit o' man-aise?'"

I cannot recall ever saying "thank you," because most assuredly the following day one of Miss Mary's sons or Miss Cynthia's kids would be knocking on our door asking if we had a couple cubes of ice, or a cup o' sugar, or a half-a-stick o' butter. It's just what we did.

Grownups placed their living room stereo speakers in the windows facing outward so everyone could hear the latest Donny Hathaway or the newest Aretha Franklin jam. It might be 10:00 p.m. on a Friday night in the middle of July; our parents would be kicked back drinking a beer and talking shit. My friends and I would be running through the parking lot, playing tag or telling on each other, oblivious to time and high temperatures. At four and five years old, we cared only about having a good time. And indeed, we did.

Skates were popular in the mid-1970s. The skates of that era each had four metal wheels and were worn over the shoe. One could adjust their skates with a skate key and share them with someone whose shoe size was different. On Christmas mornings, we wrapped ourselves in new winter coats with white fur around the face, and wore knit caps pulled down close to our eyes. Then we would ride up and down the rugged sidewalk, struggling until we were "bad" enough to twirl and jump off the curb. If someone didn't get skates, we would let them wear one of ours and both roll up and down the sidewalk, using the one free foot to gain momentum for the outfitted foot. Then we'd ride on the handlebars of someone's new bike. Aunties, cousins, and Grandma came over for dinner and there would be enough for everybody to take an overstuffed plate of food home for midnight snacking.

I had my ears pierced in my mother's kitchen by Miss Pauline who lived in the row house behind ours. She used a sewing needle that she burned on the stove and then dipped in alcohol. To keep the hole open until it healed, she inserted a piece of straw broken from our broom. The straw was an inch long and burned on both tips. Many girls at my school had those broom-straw pieces protruding from their lobes, and everyone knew it meant we were getting ready for real earrings.

My brother and I got pets every couple years; we started summer camp each June; we always got new school clothes; we had sleep overs; although we had different fathers or mothers, no one in my neighborhood considered our siblings, half; our mother tucked us in at night; we felt safe walking home from school. . . . As children, we led normal lives and had no shame in using food stamps at Mr. Willie's to buy single cookies.

Of course there was violence, but we learned to think of fights as occurring between people who had "beef" with each other rather than some random, senseless act. If you minded your business, you didn't get hurt—usually. Grownups fought over somebody messin' with somebody's man. Girls at school fought over he say/she say, as we called it. Kids who thought they were better than everybody else got beat up on the way home. Boys hit us on our butts and ran. We assumed this was how everyone lived.

In recent years, the ghetto has gotten rougher. Many convenience stores now have bulletproof glass and one is required to slide his or her money through a slot underneath that glass. The introduction of crack cocaine into the ghetto has generated a host of "street people" who roam throughout the nights and days. These are women and men who sleep in abandoned homes and wander in search of their next high or boosting opportunity. Kids tend not to say "yes ma'am" to elderly women anymore. People still put speakers turned outward in their windowsills, but now the music has explicit sexual references. Violence in the 'hood is often senseless, and what used to be cause for a fist fight now apparently warrants the use of a knife or gun. A murderer may live on a block among families; everyone knows, but no one is willing to take action.

Still, I argue, it ain't that bad.

While the ghetto can sometimes be a hostile place, I argue that it is not as disparaging as "compassionate" Americans often make it out to seem nor do the disparages which do exist dictate the day-to-day, moment-to-moment existence for the people who live there. The lifestyles of most Blacks in the ghetto pale in comparison to abject poverty, which means being close to starvation, having no access to meaningful education, and having no safe place to sleep. While crime, teen pregnancy, and hard times are rampant in Black ghettos, people who live there own jewelry, wear name brand sneakers, and eat several meals per day. Furthermore, most will argue that the ills of capitalism and racism so heavily afflict those who live deep within the inner city as to not to have any conscious awareness about them. While this is true for some, Black folks from lower-class communities distrust the system and develop meaningful critiques of and alternatives to it, nonetheless. We generate critical discourses about the White man and light "skin-ded" people. We have "hookups," people from whom we can borrow $10 and promise $15 back when our check comes. We create our own systems in the ghetto and do not see ourselves as victims, typically.

The esteem of Black people in the ghetto is much higher, I would argue, than the average middle-class American might believe. Young women with wide hips and hair so fly they sleep with their head off the side of the bed raise children with dignity. Young brothers clean their white sneakers with a toothbrush every night and do not normally turn to selling drugs. They do what they must to graduate high school or get a G.E.D. and they work on their hoopdie's until the accessories on the car cost more than the car itself. They find esteem in their sneakers, their cars, their sexual conquests. Many of them become what Marx called the lumpen proletariat, hustling mostly legit businesses, creating their own car wash services, or laying carpet, or painting homes.

White folks whom I've met, who grew up poor, have often asked why their living among other lower working-class Whites doesn't constitute "living ghetto." I've struggled to make sense of this notion and can't help but come back to how the term is defined: "a section of a city, especially a thickly populated slum area, inhabited predominantly by members of an ethnic or other minority group, often as a result of social or economic restrictions, pressures, or hardships." The ghetto is a complicated construct, and has evolved out of the unique ways ethnic people have made the best of what little they've been given. I have also imagined that since culture emerges from patterned behaviors and values people attach to those patterns, the ghetto, like food, language, and music are extensions of ethnic culture. I liken this notion to the fact that fried catfish and baked macaroni and cheese are soul food when we prepare them, but are considered home cooking when prepared by Whites.

Many will argue that the reason why Black women represent the largest group of new AIDS cases is that they are poor and have limited access to healthcare. Even when I explain that most of these new cases are from heterosexual contact, they insist that poverty breeds ignorance and this lack of knowledge leads to risky sexual behavior.

My retort is that a significant number of the Black women who contract the virus are neither on welfare nor living in subsidized housing. Many of these women are working-class females who are intellectually and intuitively aware that sex can lead to infections, HIV, and pregnancy. Even the poorest of poor people know this and have access to gossip, if nothing else. Instead, many of us believe that the men with whom we choose to be intimate will be honest enough to tell us if they have been infected. But most of them do not know, and some of them would never admit that they have been exposed. Furthermore, poor Black women have televisions and magazines where conversations and drama about HIV abound. Most Black women who contract the virus have jobs that make information about AIDS available to them. Thus, I refuse to accept that Black women are simply ignorant and ignored.

What might explain such high numbers of AIDS cases among heterosexual African American women a tad better than poverty is that an overwhelming number of their fathers left, or they stayed but ripped out a core part of their self-esteem and failed to provide the nurturance they needed to grow as healthy, esteemed young women. Thus, when we are thirteen or thirty-five, we consent to men entering our bodies, men who have regard for neither what we are truly seeking nor any remorse for what they leave behind.

CAN'T GO HOME AGAIN

"Aye Sweet Thang, you looking good Girl!" For years, this was the mantra of my father as he drove past Black women with thick hips and big hair. "Can I go witchu, Baby?" he would add, though surely he would rather they come over and lean in his car than him getting out. If the woman responded with a smile or greeting, he would add, "I don't know whose child this is," using his thumb to point at me as I sat perched up near the windshield before seatbelts were en vogue.

At just four and five years old, I felt out of place in those frequent moments of my father yelling out to strange women. I felt very little frustration for myself and great discomfort for the women on their way to Rite-Aid, or a bus stop, or a PTA meeting. As a little girl, I couldn't curb the fear of becoming those women, of feeling violated in public. I just knew I didn't like it and wanted for him to speed up and just let them be. Now close to sixty and married for the fourth time, my father is still quite easily distracted by round, brown women on the streets who no longer slow their gait or offer hints of possibility.

Between my parents' breakup in 1972 and when I left my mother's house in 1978, I visited my father every other weekend. Those were dream weekends and I was a princess with little concern about any other girl who may or may not have been loved by her king as much. I doted on my father and trusted him unconditionally. Nothing could come between us, ever, I thought.

His second wedding was in my grandmother's backyard. I was a dashing flower girl of only eight years old, but I ruined my performance because I cried throughout the ceremony. Some other person was now the center of his world and I could do nothing about it. Jean was just twenty-one, soft and homely—not at all the kind of woman one would think was his type. She lived with her parents just before the wedding, and was blissful about being his bride. I stayed close to my father during the reception, holding onto one of his legs as he walked around on my grandmother's fresh-cut lawn greeting family and friends. When one of my aunts asked why I cried, I shrugged my shoulders. I really didn't know.

My father said, "You're not going to lose me. Okay?" I nodded. That was all I needed to wipe the sadness from my face and feel free again. Before the reception ended, my father approached me and said, "You wanna come live with me?"

I jumped up in his arms and hugged his neck. "Yes, Daddy!"

I could not have been more thrilled as he carried me around for the next ten minutes, my feathery white dress now wrinkled and rife with Kool-Aid stains. Everything was right in the world after he asked me that. I was sad to be leaving my brother, mother, grandmother, aunts, and a handful of cousins in Cherry Hill, but glad to have my daddy full time.

Then I got to witness my father interact with a woman on a daily basis. Neither of them was affectionate or romantic; they never said Baby or Honey to each other or even cuddled on the couch. He convinced himself that consistently saying she was dumb was the motivation she needed to grow. She never fought back nor called him names in return. Once, during a trip out of town, my father sent Jean into McDonald's to purchase Egg McMuffins for us. She came back with *English* muffins.

He yelled, "What the hell are we supposed to do with these goddamned muffins! You are so dumb that I can't count on you to get a McDonald's order right! Shit!" He reached into the bag, pulled out the buttered muffins, and flung them individually out the window onto the busy Baltimore street. He was driving almost twice the speed limit and nobody said anything the entire trip.

She sometimes attempted to explain why she forgot to take the ground beef out of the freezer in the morning, or why she ran out of time after work and failed to make it to the market, or why her sisters said little to him when they came over every now and then. She never raised her voice and often gave up before her case could be made. She sat still as he shrieked about lights left on or cleaning that was insufficient. But she never really spoke. One Friday night, though, something in her had changed.

He had been screaming at her about who-knows-what. Hot-link polish sausages were on the menu, and unlike most nights, neither of them sat with me at the dinner table. He was in the basement, still complaining about the issue, when he heard her in the living room make a comment indecipherable to either of us, but loud enough for him to know she said something. He always had the last word on everything, so this was unusual. He was a marathon runner during those years, and when he heard her mumble, he dashed up from the basement two or three steps at a time. I felt wind rush past the side of my face as he jetted by and trampled her in the living room behind me.

"You running your goddamned mouth?" he exploded.

He straddled her as she attempted to cover her face. My neck was stiff but I managed to rotate it to witness him punch her. Once he peeled himself off her, he told her she had better not run her motherfuckin' mouth anymore.

I gawked at the plate, the sausage, the soggy bread. Everything was red and hazy. I had stopped chewing and swallowing moments earlier, and my cheeks stayed full until the ordeal was over and I could make it to the trash can. I was afraid he would notice my attempt to blink like the woman on I Dream of Jeanie and hide myself inside a corked bottle somewhere. I was not allowed to comfort her and could say nothing to let her know I understood and shared her fear. I was powerless and stuck. My body shook as he whisked past me heading back to the basement. I could hear him panting, although there was a cracked door and fourteen steps between us.

Later that night, during one of my needless trips to the bathroom, I noticed tears rolling down her face as she moved her clothes from their bedroom to the guest room. I stared from the tiny space in my door, bewildered, watching as she lay on the twin bed facing the wall. I'm sure she ached for herself. I, on the other hand, was ripped apart because I no longer had a man in my life who I was sure would protect me. The events of that night have stayed with me and affected my ability to get close enough to a man as to marry and move into a home with him. But more, the experience epitomized the secret world inside 2430 Shirley Avenue, the one my cousins and uncles never knew — the one just like that of my father's parents and my own parents during the last year of their marriage.

I never saw him hit her again, but for the remainder of my childhood, Jean and I could not connect or rescue each other, and certainly could never speak openly about what we thought of him. I was determined never to become Jean. I would always have a voice, I maintained, although now sometimes I feel like I'm seated back at that kitchen table with burning hot sausage in my cheeks and red everywhere.

Things got worse as I got older. Rather than spank me for not cleaning my room or missing curfew, he would offer a stern slap to my face. I was seventeen the last time he hit me. I support spanking children when it's "necessary," but have never believed a man should hit his daughter after she has reached puberty. It sets her up for all the wrong beliefs regarding her self-worth and rights she has to own her developing body. He never said, "I only hit you because I love you," which would have sent mixed messages, but would have reassured me that my throbbing ear, or aching shoulder, or sore lip had purpose. While the time between him hitting me might be twelve or thirteen months, the indifference he showed toward me was pivotal in creating an indelible wedge that remains wide-open today.

During the in-between times, he took me to Oriole games, helped me shop for training bras, and made sure I had humongous Christmases. (One year, I counted eighty-six items he had placed under the tree for me.) But his struggle to express affection and praise, which is the stench that lingers heavily on him even now, is what I have sought — unsuccessfully — to mend. I still long for kisses on my forehead, strokes to my hair, I love you's at the end of phone conversations . . . . What I've not gotten from him, I've sought in other men, in food, and in therapy. Given that neither his third nor fourth wives was old enough to be my mother, one two years younger than I and the other three years older, I contend that he is searching for me too.

He apologized to me only once in my life. He said he was sorry for yelling about my inviting friends to sell him milk chocolate almond bars at the school fund-raiser, during a time between paychecks when he had no money. I had come to expect these outbursts about issues I thought were meaningless. For all the things I did deserve apologies for, I got nothing. For all the things I deserved commendation for, I got nothing.

When I asked him to tell me if he was proud of me, he said he didn't want my head to get big. Throughout my childhood, I held his secrets about the other women he slept with while married to Jean. Still, no thanks. Just recently, he witnessed me pull off one of my most impassioned lectures of the semester, one focused on Miles Davis and other celebrities who beat women and are still revered by our community. I had hoped he would say he was stirred, stimulated, or amazed at my wisdom and verve. Instead, when I asked what he thought, he merely said, "I love Miles Davis."

Developing breasts and enjoying boys' attention generated a deeper rift between my father and me. He grew confused and disconnected whenever the subject came up of boys calling, coming to visit, or asking me out. He was so distraught about the idea of me going to my senior prom, he asked me to leave from my mother's house in Cherry Hill. Before I moved out of his home at eighteen, I was still not allowed to date nor have boys call. This inability to maintain a healthy relationship with my father and no permission to develop connections with boys my age would define, in large part, my emotional state for the remainder of my young adult life.

Junie was my first boyfriend. We snuck around to see each other during my final two years of high school. We carried on, in secret, as if we were the most important people in the world. He was studying to be a mortician and secretly hoped to be an evangelist. I was smitten. When I was seventeen, Junie heard some he say/she say about me. He immediately drove his mother's two-tone blue Cutlass to my father's house, summoned me outside so that I could give him his belongings, and then did the unthinkable. He reached far down in his gut for it. Believing that no future preacher would ever commit such an egregious transgression, I stood still. Then before I could get too confident in my stance, he hurled a blazing chunk of spit in the crevice between my nose and left cheek. He rushed to the car, the engine still running—door still open, and sped off. I was more hurt than angry and I felt extremely violated. What upset me most is that I could not climb the stairs to our front porch and act like a damsel in distress. Junie knew this; he knew my father would not rescue me. Junie was confident I would not tell my father who he was to me or why I had met him outside. I was on my own, and have been dealing with battles like this on my own since then.

I wish I could have told all this to my 7th grade social studies teacher, Mr. Carusi, a White man who had been working in Baltimore's inner city public schools longer than I had been alive. His voice was a soothing balm to my daily life at Greenspring Jr. High. It wasn't just that I was in the top classes throughout junior high that he believed in me. He saw things about my personality that he liked and wanted to nurture. He saw potential in me that he never ceased to mention. Mr. Carusi and I stayed close throughout the years and yet, I felt I would be betraying the other men in my life to speak candidly with him about what was happening at home.

Countless Black feminist authors have paved the way for us to talk openly about the brothas in our community who hate women. Since the 1960's Black Power Movement, it has been taboo to air our dirty laundry, to pull back the scabs and let White folks see us bleed. What has been even more unacceptable is discussing how Black fathers who are present in the home, who take responsibility for their children, can sometimes destroy their little girls' ability to see themselves worthy of honor and respect. Certainly, the brothas in our communities who make it home from a hard day at work and ensure that Christmases are always extraordinary, cannot be *too* bad. Right?

$\mathscr{B}$EGINNING OF THE END

Once when I was thirteen, my father beat me within an inch of my life. He cornered me behind the front door, pounded on me until he was tired, then yanked my whole body off the floor by my left ear. He will likely deny the details of that day. But I can't. It marked the beginning of my lifelong disconnect from men and from my own body.

One weekend evening in June my father and stepmother had tickets to see Patti Labelle. The weekend was a regular occasion when my older brother Maurice visited, and the expectation was that he would keep my company while my father was away for the evening. I left the house about 5:00 p.m. and went down to Greenspring Avenue, just two blocks away, to spend time with Squirm. He was sixteen, and had large lips and a hypnotic smile. He enchanted me although we talked about relatively innocent stuff: the neighborhood, who was diggin' whom, who was talking behind whose back. At about 7:15, I watched my father's sleek black Mitsubishi roll by. I thought very little of his leaving because I had a 7:30 p.m. summertime curfew and I was still slated to be in on time.

When I walked in the house, Maurice said he and my father had gone door-to-door looking for me. I stuck to my defense about curfew. I had done nothing wrong, I thought. It turns out, my father wanted me in the house prior to his departure; apparently, I had done something really wrong. Maurice alleged that he had never seen my father so angry and he himself feared being punished for not finding me. I didn't believe him until my father called from the concert hall delivering the stern threat that I had better not move until he got home. My thinking was stuttered and I itched uncontrollably. Leftover oven-baked french fries sat shriveled on the stove as a reminder that I missed dinner. I gnawed on them but could hardly swallow.

Maurice repeated, "We looked everywhere. Didn't you hear us calling you?" His question interrupted my attempt to generate a story that could clear all this up, save me, anything—except reveal that I was spending time with Squirm.

I sat on the living room couch, but the plastic covering made the back of my legs sweat more severe than usual. Thinking that feigning sleep would stave off being murdered, I went to my room and laid in the dark. I rocked back and forth with the pillow covering my head, barely able inhale. Shortly, I heard the roar of my name from the bottom of the stairwell.

Then I heard, "Get your ass down here!"

He had barely closed the front door as I tiptoed down the creaking steps. Just as I had used those couple of hours to manufacture intense terror, my father had used them to become ravishingly angry. Maurice scooted from the living room to the kitchen and pretended to be occupied with washing dishes.

"Where the hell were you?!" he grunted. My father asked this, already knowing there was no correct answer to the question.

I spoke barely above a whisper, saying, "I was with Shanna down on Greenspring."

"You're a goddamn lie?!" he yelled.

"Shanna said she didn't know where you were," he declared in that high-pitched voice which still unnerves me.

Before the last syllable could roll off his tongue, he knocked me into the back of the hardwood front door with one punch to the side of my head. I crouched down in the corner and screamed mercifully. My stepmother stood on the stairs, covering her mouth with both hands. Certainly, she had witnessed me get ass whippings before, but never anything this brutal. He punched and pounded.

"Oh my God! That's enough!" she screamed. He ignored her plea. I could feel his fists connect with my bones.

I may have been crouched in that corner only 20 or 30 seconds, but it felt like 20 or 30 minutes of high-powered windmills coming at me from all directions. Then just when I felt I was seconds from eminent death, he grabbed my earlobe and yanked my limp body up the stairs. As he pushed me in my room, he shouted that I had better remember this if ever I caused him to roam the streets again. I still can't forget.

The cold fries remained stuck in my throat. The entire left side of my face ached and throbbed so thunderously I could hear my pulse. Every part of my body stung, except my feet. But I could hardly rely on them to keep me balanced as I stood over the Raggedy Ann trash can desperately praying to cough, catch dribbling snot . . . breathe. I knew not to suffer loudly and invite more of the same. I turned off the light, and again sought solace under a pillow.

I could hear Charlie and Sharon, the kids next door, imitating me. They got close up to the wall we shared and reenacted the scene with a dramatic spin: *Owww, don't beat me no more Daddy. Please Daddy, please don't beat me no more. . . . Ha, ha, ha!*

My father barely looked at or spoke to me for days after that incident. My face still ached the next day, which caused me to fade in and out during breakfast as he laid out my punishment, which included extra chores, no phone calls, and not leaving my room except for meals. I could have swallowed this like a champion if it meant he was willing to extend some semblance of compassion. A smile as we passed in the hallway may have been enough. A compliment of how well I did my new chores might have even made me think he was glad that I survived. Anything. The silence and looks of disdain were more agonizing than the lingering bruises, and the meanness still haunts me.

I would never claim that my father physically abused me. He acted within the realm of acceptable behaviors for my time and my family's core values.

After one month of not being able to leave my room, my father allowed me to go outside and reconnect with my friends. I avoided Charlie and Sharon, pretending I didn't notice they were on their front porch still mocking me. My curfew was more rigid and I had to check in every hour when I was away. The following weekend I saw Squirm sitting alone on his front porch, so I sat with him. I didn't reveal where I had been for so long nor mentioned anything about the physical and emotional wounds I had sustained on our last night together. He asked me into his house for the first time where we crept upstairs to his bedroom. Red lights beamed from opposite corners and the room smelled like gym sneakers. I was tense. Squirm asked me to lie across his bed as he proceeded to suck on my neck. He worked his way down to my tummy, lifting my shirt with his tongue. He licked my belly button, but used way too much spit, I thought. My entire body quivered, definitely more from uneasiness than arousal.

Mentally, I was somewhere better as I had begun to imagine which one of the girls around my way I wanted to tell that this was finally happening. Erin, Lisa, Shanna, and the other girls on Shirley Avenue had all bragged about having sex and had teased me because I was still a virgin. Everyone except Shanna was younger so, obviously, I had to get with the program. I drifted off, staring at his posters of Jet beauties, wondering if he was disappointed that my titties weren't full like theirs. He pulled my Gloria Vanderbilt jeans down, off, and onto the floor. He slid his basketball shorts and white drawers down around his ankles then laid his whole body on top of mine, and then pierced my dry pussy. My hips were stiff as a board. I shifted my gaze on his sneakers lined against the side wall, and wished he would hurry up so I could make curfew. My face wrinkled as I closed my eyes and grunted.

He said, "You gotta relax."

After a few pumps, he climaxed inside me. I slithered from under him, got dressed, and said I needed to get home.

As we turned the corner from his block of Greenspring onto my street, he put his arm around my shoulder and asked, "You're on the pill, right?" I had not told him I was a virgin so he assumed I was on the pill like the other girls.

"No," I commented as I looked down at my untied sneakers.

At first he responded with a somber, "Shit." Then he mouthed, "Don't move."

He sprinted back to his house and reemerged in moments with a balled fist extended. He dropped two white pills in my hand then advised me to sit in the bathtub for one hour after taking them. He looked square in my eyes as he offered this prescription, suggesting it was a tried and true method for ensuring I wouldn't be pregnant. I wondered how he was able to access such a magic remedy so easily. But I didn't ask. I told him I should walk the rest of the way alone, thinking my father would murder me for sure if he saw me with a boy.

I had enough sense not to take pills that had no name. I did, however, sit in the tub for one hour trying to make sense of the pinkish discharge as it oozed from between my legs and fell to the bottom of the tub. At

13, I had not thought much about my virginity as something to be treasured. It was a curse. Virginity was more shameful than being pregnant in my 'hood, so there was no way I could think about innocence lost. I just needed my friends to get the fuck off my back.

I swore to God I would never do it again. And I didn't, willingly, for years.

$\mathscr{S}$OME TIME IN AUGUST

Big things happen for me in August. My birthday is August 10th. My first trip to Africa was in August 2001. I graduated with a Ph.D. and began my career as a university professor in August of '99. I started locking my hair in August '97. I began college in August '87. And in 1984, just one day before my 15th birthday, I had an a-b-o-r-t-i-o-n. *That* word still gets stuck in my throat.

On the morning of the "procedure," I kept staring into the mirror, turning from side to side to check my profile. It had been two weeks since I could button my pants comfortably and started wearing oversized shirts. Nausea overtook me most mornings but I denied it to my father when my stepmother told him about her suspicions. I certainly could not tell my best friend Alice who, although I trusted her with most things, would surely have told at least one person instead of erupting with such juicy gossip.

Just weeks prior to my getting pregnant, my father asked my mother to escort me to the clinic for birth control pills. She was delighted to spend "girly time" with me and was eager to do it, instead of leaving it up to my stepmother. The nurse who issued the pills at the free clinic in Cherry Hill told me to start them on the Sunday after my next period. My period did not come later that month or the next.

During this time, my father asked me how it was going with the pills. I lied and said everything was fine. He then asked to see them, which made me anxious since I had not even opened them or read the inserts. I ran to my room and scrambled through my panty drawer for one rectangle pack. Ripping through the packaging, I rushed to calculate the day and color pill that should be in the tiny window. I could not recall whether it was Friday or Tuesday as I frantically pushed random pills out the back of the foiled wrapper.

He yelled, "What's taking you so long?"

I said, "I can't find them."

That made no sense to him since I was allegedly taking the pills ritualistically and, thus, should be able to find to them immediately. When I managed to push out enough peach colored pills and position the half-empty pack sideways into the plastic container, I sauntered into his bedroom and handed it to him. He inspected the packet over his eyeglasses with his head tilted downward.

"How do they work?" he asked.

I was shivering, trying my best to summon up exactly what the woman at the clinic said. *A peach one every day at the same time, then the white ones when you have your period.* . . . I convinced him and he never asked again.

Alone, I caught two city buses to an unpretentious-looking red brick building on Edmonson Avenue. I found the phone number in the yellow pages. Planned Parenthood was not an option because my classmates went there for birth control pills and annual checkups. I was frightened about seeing someone at the Edmonson Avenue clinic, too, but thought it was far enough from my house and school to be safe. I arrived there at 8:55 a.m. for my 9:30 appointment. I signed in with the name Joanne Crawford and filled out the data sheet with erroneous information, including the date of my last period. I believed I was too far along so I listed a date that would make it appear I was ten weeks instead of the more accurate thirteen weeks. When I was much younger, I would pretend my name was Joanne. I frequently eschewed my real identity during playtime, and always ended up calling myself Joanne. This time it was for real. This time, I had hoped it would keep me undercover and safe. I also wrote that I was eighteen years old.

When the nurse called me in and requested that I pee in a cup, she told me to place the cup in the window when I was done. I squatted over the toilet, too preoccupied to pee. When finally I did, I put the opaque cup with "J CRAWFORD" on the lid in the sill of the open window. I went back to the waiting room and sat almost four hours, during which I noticed girls who appeared even younger enter and exit the office. When I asked the receptionist how much longer I would have to wait, she checked with the nurse who said she never received my urine sample. I insisted that I put it in the window and even offered to show her. When she and I got to the bathroom, I was right. The only problem was she meant the window that separated the restroom from the testing room. I thought she meant the window leading outside.

Just moments later, a short round woman who seemed ready to go home said, "Joanne? Follow me."

We marched in unison into the room where she asked me why I had sat so long without saying anything. I was trying to act eighteen and did not want to ruin it with an explanation that would make me sound immature. The truth was, I was terrified they were using those hours to verify my personal information and discuss among themselves whether or not I could have the abortion. Never looking up from her clipboard, she asked me the date of my last period, and then told me to undress from the waist down and wait for the doctor. He was a lanky White man with a long face and bump on his nose. I tried not to stare when he explained what I would hear and feel during the procedure. The woman next to him did not look like a nurse. She chewed gum and was dressed in a polyester royal blue blouse that kept drawing my attention.

My breathing was stammered and I was distracted, but I heard him twice say, "She is definitely beyond ten weeks." I was afraid he would stop and make me go to a hospital. He didn't.

In just a few minutes, he was all done. When I got dressed and taped the oversized sanitary napkin to my panties, Miss Royal Blue told me to lie down in the room next door. After just two minutes of being in the room spinning and spinning, I stood up and bent over mumbling, "I need a trash can. Somebody help me! I need a trash can."

The woman from the front desk came from around the corner demanding, "Miss Crawford, please lay down."

I vomited in the hallway near the bathroom with the two windows. I was weak! She gave me brown paper towels then walked me back to the cot. I laid there for less than ten minutes, the entire time thinking I needed to hurry up home before my father arrived. I hobbled to the front door and down the steps, assuring Miss Blue and the receptionist I would be fine.

It took some time for me to get across the six-lane street to the bus stop. I could already feel the blood spilling over the sides of the pad, so I took off the top shirt of the three I wore to hide my tummy, and tied it around my waist. I sat in the back of the bus with my head in my lap. I was queasy, still.

On the second bus, I sat in the first seat and tried not to contort my face to give away that I felt heavy cramping and shame. I stood up as we approached my stop then looked back and saw a blood stain on the blue cushion almost as wide as my hips. The bus was quite empty and I hoped the driver would not turn to notice. As I walked the five blocks down Shirley Avenue to my father's house, I kept twisting my upper body to check the dangling shirt. I noticed a large ruby-colored stain that appeared to get bigger every few minutes. Thankfully, I made it home without encountering anyone I knew.

When I got in the house, I didn't want to alarm my father by leaving water in the tub indicating I had showered in the middle of the day. So, I cleaned myself in the sink, changed clothes, and lay balled up in the center of my bed. Feeling extremely lethargic, my vision was blurry by the time my father walked in and asked why I was lying down in the middle of the day. I told him it was *that* time of the month and that I had taken some medication, which made me sleepy.

About 6:00 p.m. Lisa and Deanna, two of the girls from across the street, knocked on the front door. My father called me to the porch where they were waiting as if they were holding in something serious. Deanna said she had heard I said something about Lisa and that Lisa wanted to beat me up for running my mouth. I had no knowledge of the hearsay and told them that I was not in the mood to deal with their junk.

I was still woozy when Lisa, the yellow girl with the gargantuan breasts, stood towering over me with her arms crossed and said, "I want to fight you."

I asked her to wait a minute, and I went inside to summon my father. Under normal circumstances, I would have gotten loud and attempted to avert the fight with threats to really hurt somebody. But this time, besides having little strength, I figured that a rumble would give away my excessive bleeding, so I had to ask my father to intervene. He lectured us about getting along and sent them home.

* * *

I was an actress at an all-Black theater company when I was fourteen. I should not have interacted with the lighting director beyond what was happening on stage. Still, I liked him because he was popular and had a nice car. He was a 24-year-old, dark, short man with a perfectly round face and big belly that made him look like Buddha. He was not physically attractive by most standards. When I found myself alone with him on the top floor of the playhouse, I repeatedly said, "I don't want to. Stop. I don't waaant to!"

He kept tugging at my leotard and whispering for me to take it off, as his dry lips ran up and down my neck. I could smell him too much and can still taste his spit on my pinched lips. Pulling me into the bathroom, which was cluttered and overflowing with stage props, he lifted me up on the counter.

I didn't strike him; through my clinched teeth, I repeatedly said, "I don't want to."

The intercourse lasted less than a minute. His penis was unusually small, but the minute seemed like forever. I never removed my leotard. He slid the crotch of the black polyester suit to the side and now I was sliding it back, but concerned the wet stain would show.

He was chummy with me for a while after that. I was shady as hell. His mother had been my English teacher the previous school year and neither of us wanted her to know. She was a gorgeous, golden brown woman who wore four shades of eye shadow every single day. She always donned the fiercest clothes and multicolored high-healed shoes. I loved her and was too ashamed to tell her what had happened. Her son was the only person to whom I ever uttered the words, "I'm pregnant."

For the first couple of weeks, he was adamant that he was sterile. That lying sonofabitch had me thinking I was crazy. But I wasn't confused about him being the father, since the night with Squirm was the only other encounter I'd had, and that happened a year prior. When I wouldn't budge from my insistence that he got me pregnant, he offered to pay half the $300 fee for an abortion. I told him I had no money, so after four weeks of avoiding me, he gave me the full amount. If I had the rage in me then that I hold now, I might have picketed outside the Arena Playhouse with a sign that read, "A RAPIST WORKS HERE. YOUR DAUGHTERS ARE NOT SAFE HERE !"

I didn't fight back so I was unsure of what to call *it*. I had no bruises and I didn't bleed. I was fourteen years old and so little of the rage I harbor today hadn't even begun to fester then. Furthermore, he was ten years my senior and I was a bit intimidated and nervous about expressing the frustration, angst, and indignation I did feel. *I didn't fight back!* is a feeling that stops me in my tracks, and haunts me to this day.

I was sure if my father knew, he would see the incident as consensual sex, and would physically hurt me, thus I began to internalize this as mainly my fault. My stepmother would not have been an ally. I didn't think about the abortion much for a few years after that summer, and would spend years conjuring up the courage to even say *that* word. I have often wished for a kinder word, something that doesn't remind me of such a lonely time in my life.

During Christmas break of my first year in college, I went back to my high school to visit former teachers. I learned that my English teacher's son had been murdered. A burglar shot him when he walked into his apartment, she explained. I stood still, thinking only of his cracked lips on my neck and his scent, a combination of Murphy's hair pomade and sweat. His fingernails were unusually long and carefully manicured, and his voice was sometimes high-pitched like my father's. I showed little emotion as I remembered these things about him. I was not glad he was dead. I felt nothing.

Every year during the hot, muggy month of August, I take baths instead of showers. I sink down deep in the tub until the water is right below my nose. I imagine myself as a baby girl forced into the world before I was ready to breathe on my own. Every summer I think critically about what would have become of my life had I not blamed myself for the "sex," had I said *I'm pregnant* aloud more than once, or had I chosen to care for a baby whose face was the splitting image of its daddy.

" $\mathcal{T}$ IFFANY"

Black girls find feminism in the strangest places. Rarely do we seek it out in College 101. Almost never do we go searching for something which "has no name." Typically, we find ourselves locked forehead first with our mirrored image, realizing our attitude has taken us as far as it could. By the time we are grown, I mean *real* grown, many of us have had the blues for years. And for those of us who have not lost faith in our Grandma's Jesus, we wrestle with the promise that trouble won't last always. Now that I am close to forty, I spend a lot of time thinking about this trouble. Mostly, I think about my troubles with sex and how I arrived here, where I am today.

To make sense of issues like mine, I must first admit that I have pain and resentment compounded upon years of doing the same thing and getting the same response — yet expecting new results. I learned this definition of insanity in twelve 12-step meetings when I used to go to them for other people's issues. Many years later when I attended sex and love addictions anonymous meetings for myself, I would learn to make sense of my own issues with intimacy, fear, connection, and loneliness. I have grown up a lot since I began admitting I am powerless, and certainly, I have come a long way in terms of honing the craft of using men to make me feel special.

While searching through the Atlanta newspaper one day about fifteen years ago, I encountered an advertisement for a job. I cannot recall the euphemistic job title but the description suggested I could make lots of money doing just a tiny bit of work. There was no implication of sexual contact in the ad. Sex talk, maybe. But not sexual intercourse. Although I identified with feminism at the time, very little of my willingness to accept a sex-industry job was about claiming feminism as a source of power. Feminism competed poorly with men for filling certain gaps in my life. Mostly, I was like other young women who rejected the once-meaningful role of daddy's little princess only to find myself tied to a lifestyle of connecting with unavailable men. This would not be my first or last struggle of that nature.

I spoke to a seductive-sounding female who answered my request for information. She told me to come right over for the interview and she described her location as a basement apartment in a residential community. Curious, I went. A tall, buxom light-brown woman who was thick greeted me with a warm hug and a kiss on the cheek. Her fantasy name was China and other fantasies she donned included supremely long silky hair, grey eyes, and size F breasts that sat strong right up under her chin. She was about thirty-five years old and seemed to be aging well, although she hid her youthfulness underneath multiple layers of the wrong-colored foundation. I liked China.

She introduced me to a well-dressed White man who appeared from a back room. He was in his lower 30s, an executive it seemed. From the other side of the apartment then came another man, Pookie, China's boyfriend. He seemed too unripe to cope in China's world. Pookie was a thin, very dark man, like Shaka Zulu, but with gold teeth. I was sure Pookie had done time in the penitentiary because his disposition was defensive and pretentious like men at the Annex. She gave me a tour of the hotel-like apartment, which was pre-furnished and chilly. The art on the walls, the furniture that did not move, and the white dishes all seemed like generic props in a B-rated off *off* Broadway show.

"You'll never be here alone," she said. "Pookie will always be in the back."

I was starting to get it.

Then she said, "To prove to us that you are not vice, you have to have sex with him," pointing to the White man whose name was (John, or Keith, or Bryan). She handed me a sheer black nighty that was just my size and suggested I get comfortable. The rush was too much.

I told China I had just gotten my period but would consider the job later. She accepted that excuse, sure I would be back, because she continued to give me details about how the operation works.

She said, "When a gentleman calls the number listed in the Atlanta weekly paper and is serious about coming over, tell him our 'massage' services are $175 for one hour. If he agrees to come, give him directions to the gas station down the street. Have him call from the payphone once he arrives. Give him the apartment address only if he calls from that payphone. When he arrives, greet him with a hug and lead him to the bedroom on the right. Close the door behind you, then ask him for $175 that you will give to Pookie who will be waiting in the hallway. Pookie will hand you a condom. Only use condoms from Pookie, and be sure that the men leave after they climax once. When a man is gone, Pookie will meet you in the hallway and give you $100. Shower, then return to the phones to address other potential clients."

It seemed simple.

I thought about it for weeks. I was twenty-five and a graduate student of women's studies, finely tuning my knowledge of the macro-politics involved in issues such as sex work. Feminism does a fine job of teaching us about capitalism and power. We learn to critique masculinity, "the system," and all those institutions that objectify the female body. The movement teaches us how to redirect our anger into letter-writing campaigns and take-back-the-night marches. But what it does not do and hits a mile-high brick wall if it tries, is make us feel full within our own arms. Men and sex don't do that either, but they do take us to places of raw emotion, of feeling *something*.

Feminist rhetoric is bullshit, and completely misses the mark with helping lost girls find their way to a home other than the one that hurled them out onto the pavement. Many of us have no visible scars and no words to name the shit we wake up to every day.

Instead of teaching us how to gut it all out, feminism instructs us to cuss unabashedly or bathe in aromatherapy salts. I love the feminist movement's potential, but I can do without the bullshit.

My curiosities about meeting men who would seek something so meaningful (or meaningless) in women as to pay cold hard cash led me to unleash any fear I might have had of being attacked or arrested. I eventually called China and told her I was ready. She said I should choose a name for myself, one that was sexy and which represented the qualities of the character I wanted to portray. This was easy. I told her my name would be Tiffany. That name somehow captured the complex symbiosis of sex and innocence, being grown up and being a li'l girl. That's how I wanted to be with men.

On my first day, the other two women who worked for China and Pookie sat staring at me as I walked through the apartment. They seemed friendly but didn't say much. One was Nigerian and a bank teller by day. The other was White and married with children. Both looked very ordinary and not at all the type you might see in public and assume were prostitutes. I often watched their metamorphosis occur when a caller said he was on his way to the gas station. The rule was, if there is more than one of us available, each of us must get dressed so the gentleman can have a choice when he arrives. Both adorned themselves with pink glittery makeup and long eyelashes. The smell of curling irons and not-so-cheap body sprays loomed heavily in the poorly ventilated bathroom. I was not much for those girly extras, but I did consistently dress in the negligee China gave me.

For the entire one month I worked there, no men chose me over those women. The White woman had naturally long hair, which she bleached almost white way too many times. The Nigerian woman wore a long, thick weave that she kept tied up in a bundle atop her head, wrapped in a greasy blue and tan nylon scarf. She removed it only for the men who came to visit, freeing her Asian-recycled tresses for the enjoyment of any man seeking a little extra dimension to his fantasy. My hair was buzz cut nearly bald, and I refused to wear a wig. They were both thin and able to look sexy without a bra while for me, even then at twenty-five, going braless unveiled maturing flaccid breasts. I was growing very bored at the apartment.

I was there two or three days each week, some days alone, and some with no callers. The phones didn't ring often, and most men who did call wanted to "get off" just from conversation. I would typically use my time there studying or catching up on Maury.

One rainy midweek afternoon while I was alone at the apartment and Pookie was nowhere to be found, a short, wide, White man who appeared to be in his 50's came to visit. I was professional just the way China taught me. I placed the money in Pookie's room, and then grabbed a condom off his dresser. I had never been in Pookie's room and so I took a moment to inspect. He had two outfits hanging meticulously in the closet, one pair of white, white sneakers next to his bed, and only the necessities on the dresser. The curtains and bedspread were the same as in the other room, and nothing was out of place. It was as if he were prepared to roll out at any given moment.

When I got in the room with the rotund man, I laid back on the bed. I was not in the mood. He smelled like the rain and could not get an erection. He tried to kiss me, which was completely out of the question. I didn't ask him his name and could not relax enough to pretend that a kiss would have made the moment better.

I opened the condom wrapper with my teeth and said, "Here, put this on."

He was flustered. I stroked his chest and mustered up an occasional, "c'mon baby." He placed the condom on then laid on top of me. I could only feel his belly between us. I shut my eyes, hoping he would think it meant I took pleasure in him feeling his way around down there. I hiked my hips up closer, but still he was limp.

He said, "Let me fuck you without this rubber."

I replied, "No, I can't."

He offered to pay me more money as he steadily breathed in my ear, panting like he had asthma. I shifted and squirmed.

"Just for one minute," he begged. "All the other girls let me put it in long enough to get hard."

I didn't want extra money; I wanted him to finish and didn't want him to take a whole hour to do it. I removed the condom then gave him a hand job. I explained that I was experiencing some irritation and could still make it good with some strong strokes. It didn't take long for him to be done, but his smell and his request stayed with me for weeks.

Days later, a twenty-something year-old Black male came by. He was gorgeous and had a body out of this world. Neither of the other women was there, but he didn't seem disappointed with his limited choice. I had already told him it would be $175 when we chatted on the phone. But now as he stared dead in my face, he remarked, "All I have is $75."

Calmly, I commented, "I'm sorry. I can't get down like that."

He asked how long we could be together for $175, and when I responded, "one hour," his eyes lit up.

He said, "I can fuck you as much as I want to in an hour?"

I told him yes, because China thought it was in poor taste to tell a man he had to get the fuck out after cum'ing once. He licked his lips in an LL Cool J motion and reached around to grab my near-bare ass. This was the first time a brotha came to the spot since I had been there. The longer we stood close, the more I was trying to figure out how to work this out with Pookie and China. I was turned on and wanted to kick it. But I had to give Pookie the entire $175 and get my cut later and I couldn't imagine meeting him in the hall and saying, "This is all he had. You take it and I'mma fuck him for free." He would have said nothing, most likely, but China would have called my ass to the carpet.

I ran my hands across the swollen print on the front of his pants and requested, "Why don't you go to the ATM and come right back." He promised he would do just that.

I stayed at the apartment for three or four hours longer and he didn't return. Only Pookie came in and went out the door. I thought about him throughout the night and the next day. He would have been such an awesome reprieve from the White men who smelled of beer and baby formula.

When I arrived at the apartment a few days later, Pookie remarked that some Black guy in his twenties came by and asked for me, saying, "Tell Tiffany that Rob came by."

I said, "Okay," but was thinking, "Dayum!" I was sad that I missed him and hoped he would call again. I had no expectations of getting to know Rob. I just liked the idea of fucking a man as fine as he and in a context where we clearly wanted nothing more than that. I imagined he was going to do more than hump, hump and go. He looked like he was going to turn my little ass out.

I had five clients the entire time I worked as a prostitute. In addition to the chunky White dude, one was a White guy in his mid-thirties whose hair was cut like a marine's; he requested only a hand job and he looked sexy naked. He made little eye contact and refused to touch me when I invited him to caress my breasts. Another was a very dark-skinned Asian-Indian man who was too eager and kept calling me baby in a way that irritated me. I wanted so much to say, "Calm the fuck down and shut the fuck up!" I was on my period the day he came, and to hide that fact, I kept the lights off and requested he switch condoms twice. Pookie and China counted condoms, so I had to explain to them the story about the Indian man, my period, and the mess resulting from the two. I don't remember much about the other two clients, except the fact that they were White and wore wedding rings.

My employment there came to a rapid halt about 6:30 one Tuesday evening close to Christmas. My two coworkers and I were sitting in the living room, dressed in sweats and loose-fitting pj's when China showed up. She demanded a meeting saying she had information about somebody "fucking up real bad." I was petrified.

It turns out she had the apartment under surveillance and had learned that both the other women sneaked in through the patio door with paying clients and their own condoms — on quite a few occasions — when they were not scheduled to work. They did not report visits with these men, did not give Pookie his cut, and *had the muthafucking nerve*, as China said, "to talk to each other about it on the house phone!" She was monitoring our calls as well. She pulled a small recording device from her oversized, overstuffed bag and replayed a call in which one of them was in the apartment and the other was away, each laughing about getting over on "that big titty bitch," and also saying that "Tiffany is too 'green' to get with the program."

The Nigerian woman grabbed her lingerie and hair sprays and left before China could get most of the way through her tirade. The other woman sat next to me on the couch and started crying. China stood soaring over both of us, then began pounding the White woman's face as if her fists were hammers. China demanded the woman pull out every dollar she had in her pockets.

China then spit on the money and threw it at the White woman's feet saying, "Bitch, you stole my muthafuckin' money! If you need it that bad, get on the floor and pick that shit up. And if I ever see you again, I'm gonna whup your ass again! Now get the fuck outta my house!"

My coworker picked each dollar off the floor, crinkling the bills between her trembling fingers as she stumbled upstairs to the parking lot. China looked at Pookie, who knew better than to interfere. Then she rolled her eyes at me and uttered that was shutting down the operation. With breath she could hardly catch, she told me to take everything I own from the apartment and leave immediately. She walked into Pookie's room and slammed the door.

I never saw any of those women again, nor did I ever seek employment in the sex industry again. I do, however, occasionally allow myself to explore sex with men even when I know that we are both only seeking something out of an x-rated fairytale.

Sex and love are easy to conflate, especially for girls like me who have been "too damn grown" since we were playing house at just five years old. I had learned then to enjoy a fantasy where I was dainty and cute, and my husband would come home from the proverbial hard-day-at-the-office. We would rub pants until we climaxed or were caught. I have revisited my make-believe world often since elementary school, have learned better at how to leap out of my body when the moment or man feels like shit, and have gotten better at convincing myself it's all real—even since discovering that rubbing pants can sometimes fuck things up.

Almond Cookie

One of my most painful experiences with a man began similar to all my other relationships, and unfortunately, ended, as did many. But for some reason, Chris seemed different, playing his role so well as to convince me that wonderland was not just my big imagination.

Chris is an emergency-room physician who visited me from Birmingham, Alabama back in 2004. Chris and I met on a popular internet-dating site that requires its members to pay a $50 one-month service fee and complete a personality profile that takes approximately one hour. I assumed that any man who would agree to answer so many questions and pay the fee, was certainly ready to do the necessary work of real love. The site is also unique in that it doesn't allow potential lovers to select other potentials. Rather, the computer system matches individuals based upon the compatibility of their profiles. Chris was the first person with whom they matched me. He and I quickly made it to the stage where we leave the internet behind to connect on the telephone. When we did, it was magic.

The hospital where Chris works is an hour from his home, and he called every day during the commute. He also called while at the hospital, insisting that I listen to naïve-sounding nurses in the background fulfill any requests he had. Chris seemed different from other men who were between jobs, between wives, and between child-support payments. He was Afrocentric and articulate, fun and laid back. There was so much about Chris that could make a sister wet.

After a couple months of connecting on the phone, Chris agreed to visit me in my northern California home for Thanksgiving. Chris's visit was part of the reason I needed to perfect "the ritual." Usually, I begin right at 7:00 a.m. I mow the lawns, pull weeds, and add fertilizer that I hope will work instantly. I make sure the outside of my home, both the back and front yards, are conducive to him shaking off the world and enjoying a beer or blunt in peace. I then go to the local convenience store and purchase white ammonia and original-scented Pine Sol, the only two cleaning products I'm sure work to undo the filth of everyday life. With my chemicals in hand, I clean the kitchen, including the inside of my refrigerator and any dish that needs rewashing. I clean the bathrooms and walls. I unclog the vacuum cleaner and push it across the carpet to create neat lines that resemble fresh-greased cornrows. I take the smaller rugs outside to beat them, clean the mirrors, change the linen, and lay out my softest towels. Then when I am sure the house is cozy enough to comfort whatever calluses he is sure to bring, I bathe, shave, and spend at least two hours grooming my hair.

For Chris's arrival, I spent so much time cleaning, buying new trinkets, and moving chairs one and a quarter inch to the left or right, that when he called from the airport, I was still in the tub and in rollers. When I finally got to him, I could see him through the smeared glass, trying hard to push excitement through the fatigue. The three airplanes had taken a toll. As I got closer to him, I noted first his expensive squared-toe, camel-colored leather shoes. Women take notice of a man's shoes for many reasons, the most important of which is to respond to our girlfriends' interrogations about every detail of his presentation. He also wore a black leather jacket that seemed tailored for his boldly sculpted torso. Though the weather in northern California was mild enough for him to have worn a cotton shirt, Chris had on a cashmere turtleneck sweater that matched the color of his shoes to a tee. He was a bit over six feet tall, and had adorned himself in silver and copper Egyptian-inspired jewelry. He was sharp. I loved him already.

But I knew when I hugged him that I was on the verge of losing myself. He and I were wearing the same brand and scent of body oil, a fragrance called "Almond Cookie," which is manufactured in only one place in the world: a Black owned, female-headed business in Brooklyn, New York. I chose to wear my Almond Cookie oil because it always made me feel real Black, something like what Donny Hathaway and Roberta Flack said. Chris and I were meant to be together, I thought. He was the quintessential successful doctor, dazzling and well endowed the way every straight/bi woman fantasizes. And the fact that he was drenched in Almond Cookie, a scent that reminds me of my own skin, meant Chris would always be a part of me no matter how things turned out.

We had the most mind-blowing sex imaginable, creating words and rhythms not yet invented. What I did not say or rather, did not question, but thought was very peculiar, is why a physician would initiate unprotected intercourse with me. Erroneously, I insisted that since he is a physician he is safe. Instinctively, I knew that if he has unsafe sex with women without asking where they have been and what they have done, he is far from safe. Still, I allowed myself to be raw in all kinds of ways with Chris. Besides, I thought this was evidence that he trusted *me*.

During his four-day visit, he explored work in my small town. He was also curious about home prices and social outlets for married couples. He promised to stay in touch with Mike at Littman Jewelers who tempted us both by taking 10% off my $3500 dream wedding ring. Chris said there were no women as beautiful and conscious as I am in Birmingham, and thus he was "willing to leave the entire South to its backward, inert existence to be here" with me. Chris and I laughed, ate, and fucked for three straight days. Then on the fourth day, he shut down. He became very distant and disconnected. I asked him repeatedly to share what was on his mind. Repeatedly, he insisted he was fine. I asked if I had offended him and he said I did not. I grew sure that he would rescind the invitation for me to spend part of Christmas break with him in the South and the other part on a luxury cruise.

Chris spent his last eighteen hours in California not speaking to me or making eye contact.

He spent his last night asleep in his clothes and so far off the edge of my bed, I'm sure one of his arms and one leg were flat on the floor. I took Chris to the airport at four the next morning. He kissed me on the lips, furtively slipped a crisp $100 bill in my purse, and said he would call later.

I never heard from Chris. For days, I carried my cell phone everywhere. I had hoped he would at least return an email. That way he could explain his feelings and lay whatever *it* was all out on the line. In my messages, I took full responsibility for what I might have done wrong: served him meat when surely he must have told me he was vegan; took too long to groom his locs or perhaps twisted them too tight; talked too much about my baby brother who was sick and, unbeknownst to me, would die exactly thirty days after Chris' departure. Whatever his displeasure, I was willing to remedy it. But he never called. That was almost two years ago. A short while after he left, I had a friend in a different area code call Chris on three-way during a time when I knew he was driving home from work. He answered. When he heard my voice, he sounded gleeful and asked how I was doing.

I replied, "Did you have any intention of ever contacting me again?"

Sounding caught off guard, he replied, "Um, yeah, I've been busy getting my medical license renewed and um doing things around the um house."

I said, "Have I offended you in some way?"

"No," he insisted. I told him to call me later when he had free time. Still, nothing.

Just the other day, I sent Chris an email telling him I thought he was an asshole. I neglected to say how much money I had spent on psychiatry fees and antidepressants since two weeks after his departure. I certainly did not tell him it would be more than a year before I would allow a man to stay over or accept the gift of food I had prepared. And no way did I mention how he was the closest I had ever come to feeling like a princess whose knight in shining armor made the happily-ever-after real. I sent the email, certain he would read it but sure he would not respond. To my surprise, he answered. In sum, he said I should let go of my anger because it's nobody's fault but my own that I hate men so much—except that I act like one. I gasped! I do struggle to understand where anger finds itself when one lets it go. After all, it is not just smoke into thin air.

Anger is like a steel ball that weighs more than the body itself. It has a life. It is a pungent growth on the skin that stinks of sulfur, and tar, and two-day-old cat pee. I am angry, but I don't hate men. Alas, when I look within and admit the painful truth to myself, I realize that I have spent much of my life caring about men more than I care for myself. And *acting* like a man?! Not me, I thought, although I can't help feeling connected to Shirlene Holmes' performance piece called, "You Force Me to Act like a Man!" about an aggravated Black woman who survives constant despair and develops a strong demeanor as a result.

In his email response, he also said what I needed was, "to learn to love being a woman." When I sat with those words, which felt like skin ripped from the bottoms of my feet, I knew that Chris was right. But he wasn't right for the reasons he thought. He assumes that a successful, independent woman wants to be a man — or worse, emasculates them. He believes there is something wrong with me doing womanhood on my terms. When I re-read his email, I felt I was back in B building on C wing in the company of men who thought they knew better than I know what purpose and value my femininity hold. I was shocked at his critique of who I was since his behavior during his first three days in California seemed to be a celebration of everything that was womanly about me: my home, my body, my vulnerability. But Chris was right about my needing to love being a woman. I urge that this is a struggle for most sistas who resist going deep into the cells of our own bodies, because lurking there are painful reminders of what we lack: demureness, innocence, and white skin. Black women, especially those of us from the ghetto, learn to survive, but never how to shift from survival mode to wholeness.

Then there was last Friday. I had planned to spend the entire day writing, gardening, and catching up on Seinfeld trivia for the next pop quiz my brother would surely send through text. Out of the blue, Chuck called. He and I had only a physical relationship, but we joked occasionally about getting more serious. Chuck insisted he was a good single brotha in need of a strong woman like me. He called to say he wanted to spend the day together. I am content with his mundane company, and I know he is not the type to commit to one woman; thus, I have no real expectations of our time together—besides good fucking. To some degree, this lack of availability is attractive to me as I do not see his unstable life as a local musician conducive to a long-term relationship, and certainly, I don't want to have to evaluate my own botched drive for independence.

He had promised to spend the day with me on several other occasions, too, but did not call or show. So I knew the odds of him coming last Friday were slim to none. That is why in our conversation the night before, I said, "I have many options for things to do. I need you to be real honest. If there is a chance you won't show, tell me so I can choose alternate plans."

He exclaimed, "Boo, I want to be with your fine ass! As soon as I wake up, I'm gettin' on the road to get close to you."

It is difficult to ignore fluff about being so fine and reminiscences of good sex with Chuck. It is easy to understand why he might not want to drive three hours from Oakland to spend the day with me when I'm sure he has options for women who live much closer. I just wanted him to be different from a lot of other men, and just say so. Still, I woke up early and began "the ritual." By the time I was done, it was noon and still there was no call to say he was on the road. I then decided to phone and ask if he was on his way, to which he responded, "I ain't gonna make it, Baby. I have to pick up my son."

Chuck was a liar if I ever heard one. The number of things he has said to me that defy even the most stable rules of physics was too many to count. Strangely, I believed him when he said he was coming, but did not believe him when he explained the reason he was not was that his oldest son's mother took Chuck, Jr. out of town and forgot to arrange a ride home.

I have my own reasons for him not showing. In short, I sometimes think I am unworthy. Not too far under the surface of my confident façade, I believe I don't deserve to be a priority in men's busy lives of recording-studio time, virtual football, and baby mama drama. So, I got mad. But I wasn't mad at Chuck for doing what Chuck does. I was pissed at myself for playing out the ritual again in spite of my knowing better. I moved like lightening Friday morning, even before I had cleaned the sleep from my eyes.

That day was one of the few times in many months since I had wrung out my emotions enough to allow a man into my home. By the next day, I was still unable to let go, move on, relax. There isn't anything special about Chuck who, like other men, leave behind pieces of themselves during their few or only visits to my home. I just wanted to believe there was something special about me that would get him to behave differently.

A couple hours ago, Chuck's youngest son's mother called. She mispronounced my name and proceeded to inquire about my dealings with a man whose name I never heard. It turns out, she was referring to the brotha I knew as Chuck. She explained that she went through his cell phone and noticed a text I sent saying, "I miss you." Then she read his reply: "I swear I'm on my way." (If only she knew how those texts captured the essence of my connection to Chuck.) She and I talked for about forty-five minutes, comparing dates, lies, and sex stories. Sadly, she explained that she was home with their baby the handful of times he told her he was performing in a show, when he was really an overnight guest in my home. She had twenty-three other names of women she was planning to call to verify that Chuck was lying and messing around. Most of those women would surely cuss her out, but she was going to do it anyway. We laughed and carried on like sisters. For the first time in a long time, I didn't feel so alone. Chuck had her thinking there was something wrong with her, too.

When I think about what it means that I found feminism to help me take responsibility for own stuff, I wonder how many of us stumble into the movement angry and seeking relief rather than the more privileged who find it in a university course or lesson from mom. And when I consider how few clues feminism gives me for surviving as a middle-class, bisexual, never married, pissed off, Ph.D. poet, I feel sharp pangs in my nose like those caused by the white ammonia I swear by. Breathing then gets to be too much and I am on the verge of suffocating until I cry Uncle and promise to get real.

I'm ready.

ANGRY. BLACK. WOMAN.

I can write an entire book about anger. If I could get away with it, I'd call it, "Leave Me the Fuck Alone!" I can't ever recall not knowing anger, intimately. I have this in common with a lot of sistas.

If I were a standup comic, I would tell a joke comparing the behaviors of Black women and White women, the type of each who often appear on Maury. I would pretend to be on that wretched show to prove the paternity of a man who I was sure fathered my child. To imitate a White woman, I would begin to describe that my fiancé and I met in high school, that he was my first love, and that we lost our virginity to each other. I would begin to sob. I'd tell Maury that I have never been with any other man and was 200% sure he was the father. It would take several minutes, and lots of pauses, tears, and tissue to tell this story. Later Maury would say to my cocky, confident White boyfriend, "You *are* the father." The life would leave my body as I continued to sit in the chair. I'd be crying even harder—joyful about the news—but hurt that the love of my life would think I was unfaithful. I'd get up and hug my man.

Then I would shift my demeanor to perform as the Black woman. My body and energy would become more aggressive and expressive. I would begin to tell my story, using my hands and flailing arms to describe the anger I felt about my boyfriend who had no business accusing me since he was the one cheating on me with my cousin or sister or best friend. The armless chair next to me would have to go; I'd scoot it to the other side of the stage so he couldn't sit next to me. Then instead of explaining that we were once in love, I would skip right to the important part: "Murry, bring his ass out here!" I'd run up to the larger-than-life monitor that has his photograph next to my child's and say, "My baby got his ears, his nose, and they both the same complexion. Murry, I'm 2000% sure he my baby fawva!" I would head back to my seat and bounce up and down in it like a jack in the box, shouting, "Bring his sorry ass out here," each word pushed through clinched teeth. As soon as he came down the stairs onto the stage, I would start swinging at him, yelling for the security officers to "get the hell off me so I can kick his ass."

Upon Maury's insistence, I would sit listening to the results. When the announcement came that he *is* the father, I would jump up in his face and say, "I told you! I told you! I told you!" I would do the crip walk and wave my hands in the air. "I'm taking your ass to child support! You gon' pay me, muthafucka! Now what? Now what? Nicca!" There would be profanity splattered throughout my declaration, but they would bleep all those words out, leaving little for television viewers to decipher.

While both depictions are grounded in grossly exaggerated stereotypes about Black and White women, they are neither completely untrue nor unordinary for the hugely successful television show.

And as a black female viewer who is neither the stereotype nor the polar opposite of it, I often holler at the screen telling White women to suck it up. I think sistas give a little bit too much drama and should calm down; but I understand them. It is easy for me to relate to their rage. Always on the verge of exploding is a reality for me too.

* * *

When I worked as a residence hall director during my senior year in college, I went to the barbershop on the day freshmen were scheduled to arrive at the dormitories. This was not a good decision, but I didn't see it as the end of the world. My boss set up a forum for my peers to decide what should be my sanction for being irresponsible. As I sat before them, defending myself by saying that I had planned to be right back before the students started flowing in and how I thought the whole situation was blown out of proportion, tears sat in the wells in my eyes. Getting fired would mean the end of my tuition being waved, and I was mad. I held back the tears, for the most part. A 19-year-old White guy on my staff made the following statement — word for word: "If you had displayed this type of vulnerability before, we wouldn't be sitting here now." In other words, I wasn't on trial for making my 'do a priority. I was being condemned because I had never exhibited a version of softness my all White staff had learned to expect from women.

Just recently, I was chatting online when I called this brotha to the carpet who justified his disrespect of women by saying he is a sexual dom. I always imagined that choosing this as part of one's lifestyle meant they were still able to negotiate healthy boundaries in public. Nevertheless, I expressed how disrespectful I thought his perspectives were. His said I was showing my color, and added, "Your smartass attitude is exactly why Black men turn to White women." That statement, along with comments about Black females being high drama and high maintenance is old news. I've heard them all several times before, in intellectual and intimate conversations. It makes no sense to me that many Black men have Black mothers who share journeys similar to mine, but then they are unwilling to love us in spite of our 'tudes. Second, if the aim is to find a White woman because she is passive, then what does that say about Black masculinity, Black men's sexuality, and the expectations they hold for community building?

There is nothing explicitly racial about sistas acting up. What is uniquely ethnic is how we interpret the experience that leads us to show out. For example, when we see perky White women flipping their hair and bouncing it all around, we tend to think she is doing it on purpose as a way to say she thinks she's better than we are because she has finer hair. We don't see it as disrespectful unless she's tossing it right up on us, but we do sometimes think, "I'm gon' yank that hair outta her head if she don't stop throwing it in my face." It's a matter of perspective, a way of seeing the world shaped uniquely within race and class contexts.

But this isn't a story about White women or Black men. Nor is it a task in figuring out why we don't get along sometimes. It's my story and that of millions of pissed off sistas like me. Rage starts somewhere. If a woman is lucky, she can name the moment and time it began. For many of us, however, it seems to have been part of the first breath we took into our lungs, choking us even then. We learned to accept it.

Allow me to explain what one type of this anger looks like when it manifests. About six or seven years ago, while conducting work with Black male prisoners, I met Nadir. He said he was Dominican, which I found sexy and alluring. Later I learned that he did not speak the language and had never traveled outside the U.S. Nadir was thirty-seven years old and told me he was serving 3-5 years for a drug charge. He shared an elaborate story about being a single parent and needing to provide for his daughter. He even offered, in graphic detail, an account of his five-year-old daughter being murdered, caught in the crossfire of inner city madness. He avenged his daughter's murder by crippling the man who killed her, he said, and alleged that they never caught him for that crime. I believed him. I believed in him.

For two years, I wrote to Nadir, giving him intimate details of my dreams and desires. I never sent him money, but I did accept many collect calls during that time and I did travel from California to New Jersey on many occasions to visit him. He had a shyness about him. He was modest and had a beautiful smile. He stuttered, which gave him a sense of youthful innocence. His hair was very straight and his butter brown skin tone seemed the striking result of hours of exposure to natural sunlight.

Although I trusted Nadir, I noted in my journal that there was something about him that just didn't seem comforting to me. I couldn't name it and I dismissed it often, which I thought was an attempt to quiet the judgmental voice that wanted to see him only as a criminal. I went online, hoping to find information about him. There was nothing. I asked one of the officers to tell me more about him while I was visiting him, but she was not allowed to say anything. I stuck to my romantic notion that a healthy relationship was possible.

Throughout the second year we were together, which was his final year in prison, I purchased clothes, shoes, and personal hygiene items for him. I even bought a formal African suit for him during my summer vacation to Ghana. I sent him clippings of wedding rings from catalogues and listened as he talked about the type of ceremony he wanted. We even agreed that if we had a child, its name would be Freedom. I never mentioned to my friends and colleagues that Nadir was incarcerated; I merely spoke of him as my lover who lived on the east coast. Everyone was dying to meet him.

They released him on January 5th. I had been in Baltimore for Christmas and waited around for his release. I booked us a flight back to California so that we could begin our new life there. I trusted that Nadir was as spiritual, bright, conscious, and safe as presented himself to be. I was down for him although he got caught up in the system. As an African-centered woman, I sometimes think it is my duty to love brothas in spite of themselves, the shit they do to destroy our communities, and what my intuition tells me.

During our first few days together, I noticed significant things about Nadir. He was very nervous about socializing with people and looked to me to do most of the talking. He bathed only once in four days and continued to wear the same clothes and underclothes every day, although I had purchased at least ten outfits and numerous underwear and socks for him. He did not contact his family, which seemed to contradict stories about them being so close. His table manners were deplorable. And he looked to me for permission to do the most mundane things.

On the evening of our fourth day together, I asked him if he wanted to go with me to the store. He declined. This would be the first time he was alone in my home. Upon my return, I had to knock to get in my front door because he had secured the top lock. He opened the door then began to pace, saying I had received a phone call from a man whose name he could not remember. He was anxious and fidgety. He alleged that the male caller told him we spent New Year's Eve together. I checked all the caller ID's and none revealed any new calls. I was nervous and phoned my friend Raquel to come over. His insistence got more aggressive. Then after an hour and thirty minutes of this bizarre behavior, he blurted out the name, "Ibrahim." That's when I knew trouble was looming.

Ibrahim is a gorgeous, intellectual, sexy, consistent, honest, conscious, natural, Afrocentric, peaceful man with whom I had been intimate a couple times over the last few years. We connected during my visits to Baltimore and would spend entire days together. He is beautiful in every sense.

As soon as Nadir said that name, I understood the reason why he was being peculiar, why he had locked my front door, and why the shit was about to hit the motherfucking fan. That Negroid went into my closet, then into my file cabinet, then into my pillowcase, and retrieved my diary. He read about Ibrahim and was pissed. Unlike most men I know, however, he was too chicken to admit what he had done. Then he locked himself in my bathroom. I've known anger, but I've never been so insanely enraged that I could rip somebody's heart out of their chest. See, this wasn't just about Ibrahim. My diary was filled with five years worth of secrets that only God and I knew. It was every admission of guilt, every ounce of insecurity, every indiscretion and violation of my core values.

I banged on the bathroom door until I almost busted a hole in it. I shrieked, "Give me my motherfucking diary," until my throat was sore. He denied having it and hesitated to leave the bathroom. When he did came out, he surreptitiously tucked it in a seat cushion. I continued to yell, "give me my goddamned diary or I will call the police on you, you sonofabitch." I added, "All that I did for you and you got the fucking nerve to go through my shit?!"

Then I called the police and said, "I have a man here who was just released from prison, who just stole from me, and is refusing to leave my house."

As he walked toward the door, he repeated, "I can't believe you would call the White man on me. You called the pigs on me? That's fucked up Nandi."

"Fuck you," I said. "You ain't no real brotha. Get the fuck outta my house. Get out!" I screamed. He left. Moments later, a young White male officer came to the door saying Nadir had just stated to him that my diary was in the cushions of the couch. He told Nadir to stay away from my home, and that was supposed to be that.

Raquel arrived and as I explained to her what had happened, I got angrier. All I could think was, I had cared for and resisted judging his deviant ass; I flew across the country to visit him; I paid expensive ass phone bills; he violated my home while wearing the drawers I bought for him; I had cooked for his sorry ass; he was laying up in my bed being serviced like a fucking king; I never asked him for a goddamned thing — ever, and the Negro had the fucking balls to go through my shit! I told Raquel that he deserved to find out exactly what he read. It served his ungrateful ass right.

It is easy for sistas who grew up in the inner city to give little of ourselves, to do only what we are required to do for others. It's a natural response to protecting our emotions and not appearing meek. Like prisoners, city dwellers can smell weakness and will take advantage. So we don't wear gentle emotions on our sleeves and we learn to strike at the slightest hint of disrespect.

What Nadir did was major. His behavior was a incomprehensible violation of my property. It's not as if he ate my last piece of chicken. He read my diary and was now more insightful about aspects of my life than I chose to unveil. His behavior was a slap in the face; disrespect at its worse. The last thing you want to do is violate and disrespect sistas who already live a relatively guarded existence, but find it in their hearts to give themselves so freely.

Throughout the night, he continued to call from a payphone. At one point, I cursed at him so loudly and for so long, it was as if I were outside of my body watching someone else behave like a maniac on the loose. I threatened to kick his ass if I ever saw him again. I had never, and since have never, cursed out anyone so badly. I hung up on him repeatedly. My rage had just begun.

Given that it was January and quite nippy outside, Raquel convinced me to let Nadir sleep in my car until I could purchase a flight for him the next day. I set a suitcase full of his clothes out on the porch. The next morning, I allowed him inside to use the bathroom. I gave him his flight information and called a taxi. That was the last time I ever saw Nadir, but the beginning of more troubles.

He continued to call, begging and crying and apologizing. I got calmer and eventually engaged him in civil conversation. Then out of nowhere, he would leave as many as nineteen messages per night on my voicemail, saying I was a fat bitch, that he loved me, that he regrets thinking I could be wife material, that he needed me. . . . Soon after, I got a phone call from AT&T asking if I'd authorized more than 300 phone calls on my calling card. Lo and goddamned behold, while this bastard was in my car, he stole my card, along with my CD case, an old phone bill, and a cheap piece of jewelry. He called ex-girlfriends, my family, and me—over and over and over. I changed my phone number so that it was unpublished, and refused any mail he sent.

He started calling my office with more erratic messages. When I reported him to the campus police, they called me into the office to share something of a sensitive nature. My face cracked and hit the floor when they informed me that he had just served eleven years in prison for aggravated rape, had twelve aliases and just as many social security numbers, and was extremely dangerous. I had never felt more embarrassed or foolish. I had introduced him to my friends. I had created a home for us. I believed him.

I couldn't sleep for days. I then gathered the photos he and I took while he was here. He was almost naked on one. I got that one blown up to an 8x10 size and sent it to him with a note attached to the outside of the envelope reading, "THIS IS WHAT A RAPIST LOOKS LIKE." The cops told me that the facts of the case suggested that he broke into a woman's home and brutally raped her, but he insisted the allegations were untrue. More than being afraid, I was pissed. I wanted to kick his ass for fucking up everything, and I was sure I could do it.

Why hadn't I been able to find this information on the internet when I searched, was my first question to myself. Then I realized that he must have committed the crime under a different alias. Now that he was required to register as a sex offender, there he was, big as day on my computer screen — with the new alias Rajah Ukawabu-something. Just last week, I looked at the national registry again, and it states he is currently in custody. When I searched the New Jersey Department of Corrections website under his new name, which tells you only who's in custody and not the reason why, nothing come up. In other words, he is incarcerated with yet another alias and set of lies.

Soon after all the mess he dropped on me had happened, he began to leave more messages in my office saying he was back in California living an hour away from my home. In one of his messages, he notified me that he found his daughter. He ran into her at Kmart, he said, and had begun to rebuild a relationship with her. (Yes, this is the same daughter who was murdered.) Then he contacted the president of the university where I work and said his son was a student there and that I was using campus mail to harass his son. The anger continued to well up inside me as I refused any contact with him.

For another year, I got more hang-ups at work and late night rants on my office voice mail. Eventually the calls stopped. Thankfully, as I said, Nadir is back in prison. He wrote to me several times. In the one letter I opened, he espoused some bullshit about being a mentor to young brothas who had no direction. He claimed he was wrongfully imprisoned again, this time for defending himself against a White man who disrespected him. He added that he wanted me to speak at his funeral because I was the only real friend he ever had. I responded by saying that I thought he had a diagnosable disorder and needed medication. I added some really mean things about what I would do if I attended his funeral. Then I told him to leave me the fuck alone. He wrote back, but I refused his letters after that.

How I behaved during this experience is one expression of anger that causes people to call us, "angry Black women." Some of the most demure, kind, Black women are bundles of anger. Many of us are articulate, educated, middle-class, and feminine. But we're also ready to fight for the right to be dignified and free. We show up strong and ready to swing because many of us have found power in anger since we were girls, and we learn this is the only way. The big fights we incite and endure may be few, but the reality of our day to day lives is that our hair, our hips, our speech, and our gum popping sass seem to be a point of contention to many folks—including, and sometimes especially, other sistas. So we stay on guard, ready to roll our eyes and suck our teeth (and kick some ass) to resist being ignored and disrespected.

Unlike the White women on Maury who take this type of disrespect sitting down, drowning their sadness in a Kleenex, *we* talk loud and *we* demand to be noticed. We were never taught to own the space where we stand, only to fight if someone thinks they are "bad" enough to make us move from it.

$\mathcal{M}$Y MOTHER'S CHILD

Shaka Zulu, a South African warrior born in 1787, was best known for creating aggressive fighting strategies for war. Depictions of Shaka show him exceptionally tall, black like winter night skies, and mean looking. Shaka grew to be a man of great power, filtering much of that power into fierce aggression toward tribes he thought were his enemies. At the beginning of the 19th century, Shaka had created the most powerful kingdom in the whole of southern Africa. Shaka had been fighting since he was a child, and died much the same way he lived.

His mother, Nandi kaBebe, was pregnant with Shaka prior to marriage with his father, Senzangakhona, a powerful chief of the Zulu clan. When they did marry, she was relegated to third wife because of *her* indiscretion, and was given very little respect from her husband and co-wives. After six years of this life with little honor, Shaka and his mother moved to a different tribe where they continued to be treated poorly — Shaka for being a bastard and Nandi for having no husband. Shaka loved his mother, almost to the point of worship. When Nandi died of dysentery on October 10, 1827, Shaka adorned himself in war regalia and screamed in anguish. He resented and killed anyone who he thought did not grieve strongly enough for her. He ordered executions on the spot, and a general massacre followed. About 7,000 people were killed, and the entire Zulu clan was ordered three-months starvation. Shaka then went to attack the Elangenis, Nandi's home tribe, killing and destroying everything and taking over their territory because of their treatment of his mother and him. Nothing was left of that tribe. On September 23, 1828, two of Shaka's half brothers from his father repeatedly stabbed him to death while he begged for mercy, and then they buried him in an unmarked grave.

What this historical event reinforces for me is how the wounds exacted upon our mothers, become our wounds. My own mother, to whom I feel painfully attached, has not lived what I would consider a good life. The eldest of seven children, and her daddy's baby girl, she would find hardship at every turn. Pregnant at seventeen by a man who remains unnamed, she was forced into an unforgiving world to fend for herself and her son. Two years later, she met my father, the only man to whom she would give her hand in marriage, and whose last name she still uses today. He was discharged from the army during the Vietnam War but reenlisted for a steady paycheck and healthcare. Their relationship, which she said was perfect the first year, turned vicious and unstable when she got pregnant during their second year together. Three years into the marriage, they went their separate ways.

As much as she would love to tell a story of spending her entire life as the homemaker to one good man, no such story exists. Quite often, men would be pleasant to my big brother and me, court my mother for a short period – just long enough to make her think he was a dream come true, and then move into our tiny, two-bedroom row house. He'd become the man of the house instantaneously and without humility, forcing my brother and me to stave off pork if he was Muslim, to clean up behind puppies if he was a dog lover, or to resist making sandwiches with our mashed potatoes if he was just plain uptight.

My mother's will to challenge the supremacy of these men must have been stolen when she wasn't looking because she seemed fine with the poor sense of security they brought. During the months between live-in lovers, I could do school activities in my mother's room. She loved to watch The Flip Wilson Show in the evenings while she counted her tips from work and picked at her feet. Unmoved by the humor in that show, I would be on the floor in her room occupied with subtracting double digits or unscrambling words.

I would look up from my activity and say, "Mommy, how do you spell . . . ?" and she would always have the answer for me. However, when the next man moved in, I was not allowed in *their* room.

And in response to the question, "How do you spell" so and so, he was likely to intrude with, "Go look it up."

I always hated that response, at first wanting to say, "Mind your own business cuz I wasn't talkin' to you!" but instead I always walked away, clinching my teeth and murmuring under my breath, "If I knew where to find it in the dictionary, I wouldn't need to ask how to spell it."

I resented her lack of resistance, of which I have vivid memories from just four years old.

I was eight-and-a half when my little brother was born. Although my mother had had her tubes tied immediately after my birth and wanted no more children, she was proud of her baby boy. I went to live with my father four months later and would see little of my mother and brothers for the remainder of my childhood.

When I was ten, my father told me a story about my mother attacking him. She went to a hardware store and explained to the manager that she needed lye to unclog her toilet. Perhaps because of the looming potential of lye being used to assault someone, one needed to state a reason if she was to purchase it in the 70's. She then took the dangerous chemical home, boiled it in a large pot, and threw the boiling lye on him, causing his flesh to be indecipherable from the blue silk shirt he wore. Feeling little vindication and fearing reproach, she called the ambulance, rode with him to the hospital, and sat there next to him for two weeks as he healed. In his version of the story, her assault was unsolicited and was the primary reason their relationship did not survive.

In her account of the story, the attack was an attempt to stand up for herself. That was the first and only time I witnessed her say she fought back. She said he had been beating her regularly, bloodying her nose, busting her lips. She told me he burst a vessel in her eye once. When she went to his mother, she often got the response, "What did you do to him? You know how he is."

After a year of being called names and burying her bruises in the pillows they shared, she purchased the bottle of lye, hoping to make him stop. She told me that story again the other day, with the exact same details as when she told it more than twenty-five years ago: the store manager's question; the busted lip; his blue silk shirt. . . . The emotion in her face seemed overwhelming this time as she stared out my car window as if seeing it over and over like the repetitious backgrounds of ol' school cartoons. This time she told the story from the moment when he entered the apartment complaining about the fact that all she could cook well was liver and onions. She is proud of what she did to him that day, but still wonders, "Why me?"

Throughout the 70's and 80's my mother had a gold crown hovered around one of her front teeth. Her smile was amazing, and she kept the gold shined by using a rouge stick rubbed onto a soft washcloth and swiping it back and forth across that one tooth. She had no blemishes on her face and wore little makeup, sometimes only red lipstick that she smeared onto her cheeks by making a big cheesy smile. Occasionally, she would sharpen the nub of an eyeliner pencil and heat the tip to make it soft enough to rub across the thin layer of skin above her eyes.

During my teen years, my father would take me to my mother's job, a restaurant/bar called The

Garrison Lounge, which was only a few blocks from my paternal grandmother's home where I stayed most weekends. I was not allowed inside The Garrison, so my mother always sneaked out barbeque-flavored UTZ potato chips and a cold Sprite. She seemed excited to see me whenever she could steal five minutes from Miss Butler, the almost-White lady who owned The Garrison. I was moved by my mother's good looks, and I blushed anytime patrons who were leaving the bar took notice of us side-by-side and said, "That's your daughter? Damn, she look *just* like you!"

She left The Garrison in 1986, soon after meeting Mr. D. Mr. D was close to seventy years old in the 80's when my mother was still pretty with curvy hips and chipper red cheeks. He was a cocaine dealer, the old school kind who dressed in flashy suits and cumbersome diamond rings on his pinky fingers. Mr. D was shorter than my mother, which was obvious when he sank into the driver's seat of his white Cadillac. He convinced my mother that Miss Butler and the other barmaids were envious of her now that she could have anything his dope money could buy. He told her to quit her job and he would take care of her. She left after seventeen years of service to Miss Butler, feeling sure her wonderland had come true.

At sixteen, I was fired from my first job. I was employee of the month just weeks after I was hired at the now defunct York Steakhouse. My mother sent Mr. D to pick me up from work one night when the manager had scheduled me to close. As late night employees, they required us to trash any leftover steaks and potatoes. Instead of doing so this particular night, I put one T-bone and one baked potato on a plate and covered it with foil. I sneaked it out to Mr. D in my backpack. The following day, my boss said he went through the garbage and compared the discarded beef with the cook's report of food waste. He noticed one steak missing. He told me not to clock in, to hand over the uniform as soon as possible, and to stay away from the restaurant permanently since thieves weren't welcome there. Ironically, as things ended for me at York Steakhouse, my mother was developing a stronger connection to Mr. D.

As her addiction grew more egregious and started to create obvious changes in her appearance, she got lost in Mr. D's world. She did not love him, but she cooked and cleaned for him, and took good care of his late-night nosebleeds that resulted in blood sprayed onto the bathroom mirror. Mr. D was married but was possessive and demanding of my mother. He bought her a brand-new Ford in 1989. Being angry with her for who knows what, he had someone steal the car in the middle of the night. My baby brother, getting wind of this, decided to get my mother's car back. At eleven years old, he walked alone from Cherry Hill to Walbrook Junction, a distance that takes fifteen minutes to drive at 3:00 a.m. In the sweltering heat of a Baltimore summer Sunday afternoon, my brother strutted. He made it one block shy of Mr. D's house, where he encountered my paternal grandmother on her front porch asking where he was going.

He said, "I'm going to get my muvva car back."

She said he looked dehydrated and angry so she demanded he come inside. My mother sent a friend to get my brother, but this was only the beginning of his decade-and-a-half long fight to recapture the many things stolen throughout her life. My brother, Munch, died at the age of twenty-six from a damaged immune system, loving her deeply, but clinching resentment of her even during his transition.

I, too, resent her. Mostly I am angry about her unwillingness to admit that she has become who she is, partly due to her continued choice to use drugs. She has never admitted to me that for close to twenty years now, she has struggled with an addiction. I've heard people say that the introduction of crack into the Black community reduced the price of sucking a dick from $20 to $5. I doubt if my mother is out there like that, but I do know that she's become different since Mr. D.

Her life, her home, her appearance, and the numerous choices she makes that invite as well as rescue her from eviction notice after eviction notice, are intricately woven into the vicious community of drugs and violence where she's spent most of her life. She refuses to talk about it. She says I'm her favorite child and her best friend, but she never tells me about how marijuana and cocaine brought her to where she is today. She assumes if she says nothing, I will believe nothing is wrong. I have struggled to make sense of my own life as a woman, simply because my mother has refused me the privilege to know her as a woman.

I've thought often that my love can rescue her. Immediately after my brother's death, I wrote a tear-wrenching letter, hoping she'd be inspired. But I didn't mail it.

Then a year ago when I walked in on my mother and aunt scrambling to conceal that they had just come in from scoring a "rock," I wrote a more aggressive letter telling her how hurt I was that even in light of my brother's passing, she still refuses to shape up her life. I told her I was ashamed and that I didn't want her in my life until she got herself together.

Now close to sixty and living alone in the projects on the south side of inner-city Baltimore amid poverty and rampant murder monitored by a bright blue police light outside her bedroom window, my mother is worn out. She spends her days sleeping and cleaning, cleaning and sleeping. She spends her late nights piecing together jigsaw puzzles, picking at her feet, and looking for something to take away the pain of my brother's death, my father's abuse, and the disappointments that come daily. During my now infrequent visits to the east coast, I sit with her while she creates concoctions of old soap chips and rock salt she will use to clean the stovetop or areas around the screen door.

Her eldest son has little respect for her. At family functions, he is dishonest to her face about why he will not answer or return calls and why he doesn't ever visit when he is in town just blocks away from her front door. He does not respect her because she had men in and out of her home, and now that she is alone she seems to lead a life of little significance. What he will not recognize is that he has become a man partly due to her strained life. But, alas, he has become one of those men who promises to avail himself to her on Mother's Day or any given Friday night, who inspires her to dust old picture frames and rearrange furniture and scrub floors, but then leaves her to peek through her tattered, city-issued window shades, wondering what is so bad about who she has become that he won't even call to say, "I'm not coming."

It has been ten years since I asked a county judge to grant me the right to use the name Nandi. It means, "woman of high esteem." Given the life of Shaka Zulu's mother, that esteem is largely defined by struggle and the will to overcome it. Most days I feel more like Shaka, angry and disempowered, than I do an esteemed survivor like his mother.

I love my mama more than most people ever tried. I feel close to her because I fear that I will inherit her life, even more so than I have already. Now with missing and broken front teeth, her smile is no longer golden. But it is sincere and still begs to be noticed.

$\mathcal{B}$LACK MEN DON'T COMMIT SUICIDE

Black men don't just give up on life. We push them to the edge; and with the soles of our shoes on their necks, we grind. Until we stop breaking them down and shoving them to the other side, the assassinations will continue.

Most of us called him Munch. My mother gave him that nickname when he was an infant because he chewed on everything. My aunt Peanut who babysat him during his toddler years called him Woogie; everyone who knew him through her latched onto the name Woogie and did not question it nor tease him about it. My grandmother called him Skipper, saying he was her "little man in charge." He never allowed anyone but Grandma to call him Skipper, and she never used any of his other names. My cousins on my father's side called him Turtle because he was two weeks late arriving in the world. I always introduced him to my friends as Will. He liked that. His name was William John Thornton III. He was proud of his name, although he spent little time with his father throughout his life, and had never met his grandfather.

Munch is the only man I ever loved. And he was the only man who ever loved me, the real me. My brother was my soul mate and I was a whole person with him. I always showed up as my true self in his company. He accepted me more than I accepted myself. His love for me was unconditional and righteous. I was his favorite person, he once told me. In my scrapbooking-obsessed days, I did a two-page layout of his photos. The heading on one page read: "I can't imagine life without him." I told him that several times.

I also told him, "Everyone in my life could die at one time and I would manage to go on. But if you leave here before I do, I would have no reason to live." I meant that.

Young Black males struggle to say, "You're beautiful" to the people in their lives. They do not develop the language that girls and White boys are given during nighttime storytelling in the gentle arms of a doting grandmother. Attempts at teaching them tenderness are overshadowed by violent shoves on elementary school playgrounds and sincere threats to get beat up unless they rebuff girly stuff. *Be a man!* is the mantra of most young boys. But Black boys, in particular, are required to embrace that plus the emptiness left behind from older Black men who live only briefly then come up misplaced or murdered.

Munch came to live with me in Georgia when he was sixteen years old. He had just flunked the 10th grade in Baltimore and was on course for disaster living in the projects. He was a well-liked child in Cherry Hill, but was fated for a rough life there. I lived in a one-bedroom, top-floor apartment in Smyrna, a suburb of Atlanta. The apartment was part of new gated community with a clubhouse and spa, and the neighbors were mostly thirty-something, single White professionals. I was elated when he agreed to come because that would be our first time living together since he was born. To prepare for his arrival, I got an additional telephone line, computer software to help with his homework, and dishes that matched. I set up my bedroom for him and I rearranged the living room for myself. I told him that I wanted to be a big sister, not a mother. In retrospect, he required more discipline than I was willing to give, but I stuck to my promise not to treat him as if he was my child.

We cooked together, giggled relentlessly, and became best friends. Strangely, we didn't touch much except for simulating WWF wrestling moves and picking in each other's nose. We got along remarkably well and never argued, except for the couple of times he had his male friends over while I was at work, during which he removed all traces of my intimacies with women. On a few occasions, I noticed my say-yes-to-safe-sex pictures of women's breasts touching, in a kitchen drawer and the framed photo of Cheryl and me face down in the umbrella case. He said he was not ashamed, but that he didn't want his friends to feel uneasy.

I said, "When your friends start paying my rent, then you can give a daggone about what they think of me."

Throughout his life, my brother never heard me cuss.

I sent him back home in the middle of the following school year. He was doing a sub par job in school, in spite of my surprise visits to his classes and threats to take away his job at the mall. I had written up a contract stating that if he was doing poorly in school when his 18th birthday came, he would have to leave the South and return to my mother's home in Baltimore. He refused to sign the contract, and it sat on his desk for weeks. Three days before his birthday and one day before report cards were issued, he packed his clothes in sturdy black trash bags. He wrapped his 19-inch television with a bedspread and taped it in more than ten places. I was disappointed, but acted as if I didn't notice he was preparing to leave.

When his report card arrived with two F's and a series of C's and D's, I was hurt. Neither of us had said a word. He purchased a plane ticket and was slated to depart on his birthday, January 24th. I drove him to the airport along with his bags, his custody papers, and his television with the busted remote taped to the side. We feverishly fought back tears, turning our heads to sniffle and massage our eyes. Our hug was fuller and less playful than usual. When I arrived from the airport to the Smyrna apartment, thinking I'd be eager to reclaim my bedroom, I felt like shit. I was responsible for whirling him out into the streets of Baltimore, a Black adult male with few marketable skills and no high-school diploma to boot.

I had committed a grave injustice against him. I felt like I had become my aunt Peanut who babysat him when my mother worked at the Garrison. My aunt was sadistic then. She would smack him for no reason and then hug him when he started to cry.

She would say, "Awww Woogie, you want your aunt Peanut? I'm here, Bayy-bee." She wanted to be needed. She would beat her own son, too, typically more than what he required to behave. But she never embraced him afterward, nor nursed him back to a feeling of wellbeing. Her son, Shawn, has been in and out of prison for the last nineteen years, with less than two years of that time on the streets. Aunt Peanut accepts much of the blame for his unstable life, but is now too feeble to make amends.

She used to baby-sit my big brother and me when we were in elementary school. She was sassy and smoked reefer. Her home was decked out with black-light velvet posters and shimmy beaded curtains. She also lived in Cherry Hill, next door to my grandmother and just four blocks from our house. On at least five occasions, once on the front porch, she beat me in my back so hard and for so long that blood shot from my nose in clots. She did it, she remarked, because I was "too motherfuckin' grown."

About three years ago, while sitting at my mother's kitchen table, she asked me if I recalled her banging me in my back sometimes. Then she asked how I would respond if she were to do it now.

"I would whip your ass," I said. I was taught never to curse in the company of my elders, but I was for real.

She looked cockeyed at my mother and asked, "Did you hear what your daughter just said to me?"

My mother gets eerily quiet when she knows I'm dead serious, so she looked away and said nothing. I turned my head slightly to the side, lifted one brow, and perched my lips. I didn't blink. I focused my chilly gaze on Aunt Peanut and said, "I'm a grown ass woman. You put your hands on me, and I will fight you like I don't know you."

She needed my baby brother to love her; for my cousin not to look so much like the married man next door; and she wanted me never to become like her. My mother's sister is now virtually homeless and struggles with gin and crack. She sells boosted items and walks the horrid streets of Cherry Hill in the snow and freezing rain. Occasionally, she is frank about her hard life; she apologizes profusely and freely exposes her own sense of victimization. She was born and raised in the projects and has never lived anywhere else except Cherry Hill.

During the final years of my brother's life, he would drive by my aunt walking the streets around 6:00 a.m. on Sunday mornings, dressed in the same meticulously ripped yellow dress or sheer curtain-turned-party-gown as the night before. She always wore bright red polish on her fingers and feet, and almost never wore a bra. He would stop to ask where she was coming from or going. She would summon up a smile, revealing her second-generation gold tooth now among false fronts.

"Woogie, I'm aiight," she would say. Go 'head. I'mma see you later."

He was enraged and humiliated, but wanted to care for her in spite of her refusal to be the type of aunt on whom he could rely for a birthday card or Blockbuster nights. He wanted to liberate her from the streets. But even after more than a dozen trips to detox and rehab, she preferred men who flattered her and bought her drink tickets, over the requests and frustrations of my brother. She enjoyed life under the influence and had no shame in begging for eighty-five cents or two dollars at 6:00 a.m.

Throughout the day of his funeral, she pushed a close mouthed smile through her steady stream of tears as she carried around a half-used bottle of fire-engine red nail polish murmuring, "Woogie hated this color on me."

Three weeks before he died, I asked him to answer the following question: "If much of the illness we carry in our bodies is linked to stress, what percentage of yours has Mama's and Aunt Peanut's name on it?

He said, "Ninety percent."

All I could say was, "Geezus." Munch wanted so much for those sisters to clean up their lives and stumble onto meaningful paths sans men and drugs. He lived with my mother until he was twenty-five, although he had long-term committed relationships with women and had a baby girl to care for. He cited the need to defend my mother in case something happened.

And something always happened. . . .

By the time he moved out of my mother's house, just three blocks up the street, he and my mother had developed a codependent relationship. Munch's girlfriend of two years treated her with respect, but disliked that my mother continued to baby him. Rita felt like it was her job to care for him now, and neither of them gave him the space to breathe.

Several hundred people attended my brother's funeral in 2004, and as is common, no one had a negative word to say. Unlike most funerals I have attended, I felt the ubiquitous honor and respect for him was a true reflection of his kindness in spite of how unkind the world was to him. He died one month and one day before his 27th birthday, instead of instantly after his 35th birthday as he said he would. He insisted thirty-five was ancient, but that my grandmother was an exception since she chewed gum and told him to "chill out" once.

My brother left behind one child, Destiny, a 6-year old mischievous child who behaved like a princess on the day of his funeral. Certainly she loves him her way, but will never know how beautiful and amazing he was aside from the stories we'll tell her and the video tape collection I cherish.

The presiding minister asked the nearly 500 attendees of the ceremony to stand throughout the church if they had words to share. Only two people spoke. The first was his estranged second cousin from his father's side who stood to say he was speaking for my brother's father, who could not make it in town because of snow. He said my brother made their family proud, and he consistently called him "Man," a moniker given by his father at birth. He spoke very abstractly of Man, which seemed fitting since he had never met him.

Then, instead of standing in the place where she sat, my brother's supervisor went to the pulpit and read from a script she had prepared. She was very light skinned with freckles and a strong south Baltimore accent. She must have grown up around poor White people, which seemed out of the ordinary because it was only recently that Blacks and Whites lived in integrated neighborhoods within city lines. She called herself his "mom away from home," and added that he was a hard worker who she encouraged to rest on the job so he could feel better. She commended herself for taking such good care of him. She was lying! That freckled lady had threatened to fire my brother because she didn't believe he was sick. He told me she refused his request for a medical leave of absence, which would entail his position staying available and his healthcare remaining effective. In America, we think it is bad mannered when people speak negatively of the dead. But I find candor refreshing, and wish people would just tell the truth already.

My baby brother is buried at the Martin Luther King Memorial Cemetery, a Black owned piece of land about as far from Cherry Hill as one could be laid to rest in the Baltimore area. The plot I selected sits atop a hill, overlooking a vast green field. The grave marker that I purchased for him has his full name in bronze above my mother's first, middle, and maiden name. Right now, no date of death is etched into the brass for my mother who is certain she will be with him again.

Tomorrow I have an appointment at Forever Tattoo in Sacramento to have my brother's portrait permanently etched onto my body. I've delayed so long because of the high cost involved, but now that it's definitely going to happen, I've been thinking mainly of the pain. It's going to take about three hours. Since I already have four tat's, I know it will hurt tremendously. But when I think about the pain my brother endured to bring so much joy to the earth, three hours at Forever pales in comparison. I welcome it.

I am not responsible for my brother's death. But I could have done more to help the man who was my best friend and soul mate. I could have written letters to his doctors to insist on the type of care they give to rich people. I could have allowed him to stay in Georgia. I could have demanded that my mother, and my aunt, and his father, and his boss, and his girlfriend, and my big brother, and my cousins, and his teachers uphold his civil rights — namely his right to live. I could have fought for him when he was too frail to fight for himself.

My psychiatrist insists that my resistance to intimacy stems from a fear of never finding a man who will love me, completely and unconditionally. I insist that such a man no longer exists.

$\mathscr{A}$ MILLION MILES FROM VEGAS

For my birthday two years ago, I traveled to Las Vegas, Nevada to see one of the famous Cirque du Soleil shows. I stayed at the gorgeous, grand Luxor Hotel. Like the New York-New York, Caesar's Palace, and Venetian hotels in Vegas, the Luxor is a theme hotel, purportedly capturing the essence of Luxor, Egypt. Designed as a pyramid, the 30-story hotel has a sphinx statue in front almost as tall. With its souvenir shops, its Egyptian-themed restaurants, and its casino waitresses adorned in gold slippers, one potentially feels she is getting an authentic Egyptian experience. That is, except for the fact that Egypt is a third-world country and the city of Luxor is rife with alienated children and old women begging for money, villages alongside the Nile that lack clean running water, and trash-filled gravesites that have become people's homes. Luxor and Las Vegas are actually 7,686 miles apart, not one million; but their stark contrasts make them seem so.

I spent two weeks this past summer studying Egypt. I stayed in Luxor for four days. I abandoned my tour group for much of the trip because daily tours of temples and tombs are less exhilarating than spending time with native Africans. While in Egypt, I noticed several striking things about the culture. First, people there typically do not state "African" as a core descriptor of their identity. Second, members of the nation who are authentically Nubian do not worship the Nile, per se, nor do they adorn themselves in red, black, and green—colors that have come to signify pride in Africa for Blacks in America. Finally, unless they were selling alabaster statues or woodcarvings, I never heard the locals mention Nefertiti, Osirus, Isis, or any of the many Rameses who ruled at some point in Egyptian history.

While in Vegas, I instinctively felt I was not having an African experience, yet I had subconsciously internalized the belief that real Egyptian women do adorn themselves with asps and belly dance waist chains in public. In reality, Egyptian women are veiled, most of them in all black to symbolize their status as married or widowed. Because the women covered their heads, I was unable to observe if they wore dreadlocks or teeny-weenie Afros like those of us in America do to show pride in being African. I doubt it.

I was astounded. I expected Egyptian men to greet me with, "Hotep, my sister, African Nubian Queen of the Nile" just like conscious brothas at Amiri Baraka/Saul Williams poetry performances. At most, the locals called me "Cousin" when they were yelling over other salesmen to get my attention; but even that shifted to "angry American" when I ignored them. African-centered Black Americans have embraced the ritual habit of referring to each other as "brotha" and "sista." But in Egypt, we are their cousins, and a close or distant one depending on how much money we are willing to spend. I was also stunned to find that at many of public places where we traveled, Arab women were stationed outside the bathroom, expecting to be paid tips for the use of toilet paper they pulled from the stalls. Unlike the employed matrons in Las Vegas hotels who offer hair spray and tampons for a set (albeit extraordinary) fee, the Egyptian women at these restrooms seem not to have been hired, but rather to have carved a niche in the strained economy, creating jobs for themselves where no job had existed.

I had not expected that police officers would solicit money in exchange for watching my back while I was on a public phone, even when I was standing next to my own male escort from the tour group. I found it disheartening that very young children made elaborate carpets without compensation, some that cost consumers up to $15,000 U.S. dollars. The trash throughout Egypt seemed the result of there being no organized garbage collection or dumpsites. I understood all these manifestations of global inequality from an intellectual standpoint. But, alas, I struggled because as an African-centered Black American woman I had been identifying with a social discourse about an *almighty Africa!*; but found very little of what I was taught to expect.

While at a wedding I encountered on the west bank of the Nile in Luxor, I was made to sit in a large room full of women. All the women beyond puberty were veiled. I was fortunate enough to sit next to a woman who could speak English well. She was twenty-four years old and had beautiful grey eyes that looked like glass marbles. The commotion outside the room and the children running in and out made it difficult for us to hear each other. During the hour and a half we were required to be in the room, she and I connected. She said she had been married for three years, had three children, and was sad that women are not permitted to work. Much of the conversation about her centered on her children and husband. I, on the other hand, talked about my life as a professor and my excitement about traveling abroad. I added that I had no desires for children and a husband, as it was one of the many questions filtered through her by non-English speaking women in the room. The women with whom I sat until the men were ready to receive us were enamored with my hair, and stood in line to touch it while expressing to my English-speaking sister that I was attractive. This was the only time I really felt beautiful while in Egypt.

Those who were unmarried wore colors like tan and dark blue, while that evening I sported an ankle-length, hot pink Egyptian dress with intricate embroidery and an open neckline that I had purchased earlier that day. My gleaming freshly-twisted locs draped around my neck and shoulders when I turned to greet children and elders who had heard a stranger was there. I really wanted to ask the young woman next to me if she was happily married, if she felt free, if she felt like she was a whole person outside her marriage and role as a mom, and whether she felt she had a voice that would be heard if she made demands. But, I did not exercise such invasions of my sista's cultural humility. Besides, it would be boorish of me to define other women's freedom by my standards.

Le Meridien, the hotel where I stayed in Luxor, is a four-star establishment. When I stood on my hotel-room balcony, I was less than 100 feet from the Nile River. Like the front entrance of every upscale hotel in Egypt, police armed with shotguns heavily patrolled this connection to the outside world, not at all a romantic notion.

On one occasion, I attempted to bring a guest to Le Meridien. Monsor is a 30-year-old merchant and native of Luxor who had initiated a conversation with me earlier in the day by asking me to help him understand the phrase "according to." I spent the afternoon listening to Monsor tell me about the local economy and social politics behind the tourist glitz. Then I asked him to escort me just one-half blocks to Le Meridien where I had hoped to creep past my sleeping roommate to grab my laptop computer and then meet back up with him in the open courtyard of the hotel. I had not paid much attention to the security officers at the front door of Le Meridien until this night.

Monsor was tremendously nervous and kept repeating, "I no speak. You speak. You speak." Although he was dressed in Western-inspired clothes, blue jeans and white-collared shirt, Monsor had dark features and cheaply made flip-flop shoes that made it obvious to other Egyptians that he was one of them.

As we approached the front door of the hotel, the armed guards rose to their feet and said, "He cannot come in."

I implored, "But he is my guest." My pleading turned to indignation because it made no sense to me that they would not consent to him being there. They did not explain the reason he wasn't permitted into the plush, linen-scented palace, so I asked Monsor to explain. He struggled with English to explain that he was not allowed inside the hotel because he is Egyptian. This notion was foreign to me. After much stagnation between the guards and me, they allowed him to sit inside the lobby on the chair closest to the front desk. They made him leave all the contents of his pockets with them, including the few pounds* and U.S. dollars he earned that day.

During the entire thirty or so minutes that we sat going through photos of my family and my home in California, the guards ogled, whispered among themselves, and tapped familiar melodies on their shotguns. I was offended for Monsor, who would not focus on the conversation or mini slide show. I imagined he felt like a second-class citizen, perhaps much the same way my parents must have felt when they attempted to navigate their way through local parks and hospitals in the U.S., the home of their parents, grandparents, and great-grandparents. I was aggravated, but now keenly aware of my privilege. I had done nothing to earn the honor of being able to mosey through their metal detectors that beeped like crazy whenever I got close, except being born American. For the next couple of days as I entered and exited the hotel, the officers' gaze shifted from civility to contempt, as if by befriending a local I had soiled my status as an American and a human being.

The next day I sat with local salesmen who, as is tradition throughout Egypt, spend most of their time leaning in rickety chairs chain-smoking American-made cigarettes. The young men were captivated with my companionship and had many questions about sex and being rich. Egyptians assume most Americans are rich. Relatively speaking, we are. But I sensed their understanding of rich was akin to what they saw on MTV Cribs, The Cosby show, and 90210 reruns. It is true that I live an extremely privileged life as a university professor and homeowner, yet I resented being stereotyped as rich. I am not wealthy by American standards, with my being so weighed down in student-loan debt and living paycheck to paycheck. But also, I am proud of my lower working-class roots and did not want to be lumped into a category with people I still think of as uppity, selfish, and out of touch with the streets.

Local businessmen with whom I developed even a bit of rapport all wanted to talk about sex. Having had this scenario play out at least twice every day during my visit to Egypt, I feel it's fair to say that they hold assumptions about American women being sexually available. Part of what that availability means to them is that we are willing to converse freely about what we do in bed and offer them suggestions for how they can get their wives to be sexually open. On two separate occasions, I had men paint henna tattoos on my hands. Given the intricacies of the designs and the time they take to dry, I chatted a while with these local artisans and on both occasions, they asked: Are you married? Why not? Do you have babies? Why not? Do you have good sex?

On my third day in Luxor, while kickin' it with the men outside Monsor's shop, Hgag sat too close to me. Hgag is Monsor's refined, classy cousin whose imported shoes and British accent probably made him popular with women. He was intrigued with how white my teeth are, and kept getting close to my face to inspect, until he eventually asked if he could have my toothpaste. As the evening and conversation progressed, Hgag kept touching my thighs and shoulders. After forty-five minutes of scooting back and shifting my body, I told him I was uncomfortable with him sitting so close and touching so frequently. He said we were friends and that he meant no harm. But his efforts at physical intimacy, coupled with questions about whether I enjoyed anal sex, made me quite ill at ease.

I changed the subject numerous times and would occasionally shift my body and cross my legs. Although I wore long pants, Hgag knocked my legs uncrossed. With the smile wiped clean from his face, he told me I was being disrespectful to him. I offered no comment. I did it two or three more times because crossing the legs for women in America serves as both a convenience and a habit. But more, it is a way we subconsciously take up less space. In either case, I thought it was strange that he would see my behavior as enticing and thus disrespectful, while he aggressively tried to elicit details about my sex habits.

With each carriage and taxi ride through the crowded streets of Egypt, I encountered men like Hgag who had strong convictions about how I was supposed to conduct myself, yet violated what I had learned were standards of decency. On my last day in Luxor, while walking past the shop where Monsor and Hgag worked, they asked me where I was going. I told them I was on my way to the marketplace. Hgag told me not to go alone. I told him I wanted to, as I was curious about how an American woman would experience an African open market on her own. He demanded that I wait for one of the men from the shop to have free time, but I continued to walk and ignore him. He scurried behind me, snatched my upper right arm, and swung my whole body around.

"Why don't you do what you are told?" he asked, as though it were more condemnation than inquiry.

I told him that in America I don't have to listen to a man and would not tolerate his orders just because it was his country. I was already frustrated with how inappropriate he had been and his unwillingness to stop when I asked.

With his strong English accent, he wrinkled his face and roared, "Get the fuck outta here, then, you fuckin' bitch. Don't ever talk to me again!"

With his arms flailing as he walked back toward the shop, he grumbled in Arabic what I'm sure was profanity and derision.

I proceeded to the marketplace on a horse-drawn carriage, pissed and fighting back tears the entire way. I am still unsure if I was hurt by Hgag's disrespect or if I was taken aback at not being able to find the reverence I had heard so much about at the Apache Spoken-Word Café. For much of my time in Egypt, I contended with shop owners who offered to sell me items at a good price if I would kiss them on the lips, or who would rub their hands across my breasts and ass and pretend it was just to make sure a blouse would fit properly. All of them told me I was beautiful and they could see themselves marrying me, but none of them convinced me that their interest was genuine. They were not as suave as American brothas who can sometimes woo a woman's panties down to her ankles like a swami with a magic flute. Besides, I had had so much experience with American men, sexually and socially, that I had developed a radar for bullshit. Their game was whack. These men were sexually repressed and wanted me to act like American "girls gone wild."

Through popular Black American social discourse, I had learned to think of Nubia as a place, a state of mind, and a culture that was consciously rich—in spite of the degree to which its land had been pillaged. In America, the word Nubia conjures up visions of beating drums, nappy hair flailing, and names like Nzinga, Brotha Ra, and Queen. On a visit to a Nubian village, I learned differently. Nubian people are from the southernmost regions of Egypt and the northern regions of Sudan, and they live quite differently from what we imagine.

The tour group took a ferry to the village, which was about thirty minutes from our hotel. The tour director asked us to bring educational materials and healthcare items from the States to give to members of this village. As our boat approached, we could see children and married women on the shore. On the side of a nearby building was the word, "Wellcom" written in fading white paint. As soon as we stepped off the boat, someone within their group shouted an Arabic word, and the children rushed us. They grabbed on our clothes and pulled at the packages we carried. Teen girls held beaded jewelry up to our faces and repeated, "one dollar, one dollar." Aly, our tour guide, directed us to the school where many of the village's children were sitting and singing, "Frere Jacque." The children seemed intensely distracted by our rolling suitcases and oversized plastic bags, and we could barely hear the murmur of French rhythms as we began to unpack.

Aly told us to pour the materials out onto tables and *he* began handing them to the children who were now in a line from youngest to oldest. Frustrated that he was attempting to be a hero to the villagers, we asked Aly to step aside and we began to give the gifts. The older children and their mothers toppled the young ones and began to rip the items from our hands. Some of them jumped on the tables and knocked over books and Band-Aids. Younger children cried and sought solace in their fathers while the taller children and mothers hid coloring books behind their backs with one hand and snatched Crayola chalk with the other. I could no longer stand the stampede and decided to leave the vortex and back off into a corner.

Once the gifts were gone, Aly broke us into small groups and asked that we follow various women to their homes. I was in a group of eight who walked briskly across a large dusty field up an uneven winding hill between small clay homes and camels. Aly had told us before leaving the hotel and again while on the boat to give money to the women because they were very poor. According to Aly, the woman who I was following had recently lost her father, her son, and her husband. Upon arriving at her house, I was shocked.

She lived in a two-level home with four bedrooms, a kitchen, a living room, and two full baths with cobalt blue tiles on the walls. Her kitchen cabinets, which had glass fronts, were stocked with food. In the living room where she served us Coca-Cola from the freezer, she had an air conditioner in the window, a satellite receiver connected to the color television, and a stacked china closet. There were three beds outside on the roof, all freshly made with matching linen. Each bedroom had two twin beds with colorful Disney bedspreads and stuffed animals. We were stunned by her home but did not hesitate to give her fifty pounds ($8) each anyway. She was gracious and seemed grateful. As we were leaving, several of us noticed the widow and Aly in the kitchen locked into a huddle. She was giving him "his cut" of the money.

As we made our way from her home to the boat, an entourage of young women who had been waiting outside the widow's dazzling home followed with beaded necklaces. There were two of them on each of us. They chanted as if rehearsing, "one dollar!" since they were old enough to speak. I purchased six handmade items from a girl who might have been eleven or twelve. None of us stopped moving as we shopped or waved them away. When the young girl fell a few steps behind me to corner my roommate, a tall woman in her 40's came out of nowhere. The strain in her quickly aging face told me she probably had a difficult life. She gestured for food money, the dual motion of cupping one hand and using the other to mimic eating. She walked next to me so tightly that I kept stumbling on her feet. Her voice trembled, but she managed to put force into the word, "Susanna," which she must have said more than 100 times with few breaths between. For most of the hike down the hill, I endured this woman attached to the elastic of my sweat pants, hoping she would give up before I gave in.

I felt they were manipulating me I and did not want to give away anything else. Since I had hauled a sac of learning materials from California to this village *and* gave the widow (and Aly) money *and* just purchased jewelry from a young girl *and* had paid extra for gifts when shop owners offered a sad story *aaaaaaand* had been scammed out of $20 U.S. by a carriage driver the day before, I just wanted to leave without anyone asking for anything else. "Susanna!

Susanna! Susanna! Susanna! Susanna!" was getting to me. I believed it was her attempt to say, "Cousin." I gave her two U.S. dollars, which she snatched and tucked away. She caught one of the other groups coming from touring another house. I could hear her uttering "Susanna" in the distance, trying painfully to say what she thought would make my fellow tourists feel like they were family.

Over dinner that night, my roommate, who is a psychology professor said, "I'm not sure who was being pimped, them or us."

Later, I asked Aly how often he takes tour groups to that village. Every ten days," he said.

The Nile River is a murky obstruction for the thousands of poor people who must pay to cross it every day for work. Jobs are scarce in most parts of Africa. Robbers from all over the globe have stolen the material legacies of our pharaohs and queens, and have left busted temples, dirt, and graffiti. From that, we create romance rife with tangible sunsets and eight feet tall kings who still walk the earth. But we forgot to tell the truth, the painful truth about Africa.

Susanna! Susanna! Susanna!

$\mathcal{S}$PEAK INTO THE FIRE!

When I was in fifth grade, two major things happened in my life. As a new student at Dr. Martin Luther King Intermediate School, I was cast as Alice in my school's production of *Alice in Wonderland*. Within days of opening night, I went from an unknown to a child pegged as having immense potential.

During the play, I was to recite a line about how my shoes are shined with blacking on land and with whiting in the sea. I wore black shoes the first two nights so getting through the line had been easy. On the third night, I wore my favorite red shiny shoes with the gold buckle.

With all the conviction of an Alice curious about her amazing wonderland, I looked down wide-eyed at my shoes, then at the turtle, and belted out, "my shoes are made with redding." I laughed so hard, I could not make it to the next line. "Redding! My shoes are made of redding!" The audience did not know the original line or the reason I was torn to pieces. My fellow cast members knew Mr. Bullock, the drama teacher, would kill me for the divergence, so they stood frozen, watching me crack up. I was alone in my deviance.

Later that year, Mrs. Hicks chose me as a finalist for the annual MLK oratory contest. Baltimore natives have a distinctive way of pronouncing words like "dog," which comes out sounding like *dug*, or "sink" pronounced as *zink*. Mrs. Hicks was uncompromising when it came to students pronouncing every letter in "mar-Tin-lu-THer-king-JOON-yer" instead of *mar-fin-loo-fer-king-jin-yer*, the way many of us said. She liked that I spoke well and gave her no reason to be repetitive in her demands. I had memorized his Selma to Alabama speech by listening to my grandmother's worn album. I came in second place to a petite, bald girl nicknamed Twiggy who made her voice quiver in a way that I thought was dumb. Dr. King didn't talk like Twiggy! That year, I won the first of many trophies I would earn in my lifetime, just for speaking. From these two events in fifth grade, I learned I could be rewarded for talking, but that I could not take the privilege of a captive audience lightly.

In 1987, I was a first-year undergraduate student at St. Mary's College in southern Maryland, which at the time had less than 100 Black students. During that year, the slogan, "it's a Black thang, you wouldn't understand" helped sell thousands of T-shirts and was woven into popular lingo. I owned a shirt with the slogan on the back. On the front was the batman logo enmeshed with a diagram of Africa. Admittedly, it was an odd design, but somehow if you were Black, you were supposed to get it. I wore the shirt while in the audience of a campus play. A White student then wrote a letter to the school paper commenting that she attended a show and sat behind a Black student who wore an offensive shirt. Oh shit, that was me! She described the shirt and expressed irritation about my sitting in front of her, believing it was the same as my screaming that she was not welcomed to explore Black culture, and shouldn't even try.

The following week, I rebutted. Far from being a great writer, I did the best I could to tell the community of almost all White people that they could not begin to comprehend what it's like to be Black in St. Mary's County or in America. The tone of my editorial suggested I wrote it with a hand on my hip and a rolling neck. I was irritated by the fact that the White woman didn't just ask me at the show what my shirt meant to me, so I could have given her a piece of my mind right there and been done with it. That's how we handled things where I was from. How dare she take issue with me and tell a thousand other people instead of saying it to my face?

That news story began a whirlwind on campus, with my politics at the center of the storm. I was a racist, some White students remarked. Black students generally sided with me. The tension on campus was thick as smoke. The debate culminated into a panel discussion the following month, which included the White woman from the play, Lucille Clifton (one of only two Black faculty members at St. Mary's), the president of the Black Student Union, the student government president, and me. The forum was in the then tiny student union, downstairs in the study area. People leaned against walls, sat doubled up in chairs, and tucked themselves into windowsills.

The spotlight was on me to offer an insightful, provocative analysis of my choice to wear the shirt. Truthfully, when I purchased it, I had not thought critically about essentialism, the notion that those most exploited by systems of oppression are the only ones who can know the intricacies of those systems. But now I was front and center, asked to set off the dialogue with something deep. I gave them fierce attitude, but was adroit and articulate. Cameras flashed. Heads shook and nodded. By my own standards of today, what I offered then was not that profound. Somehow, though, I conjured enough of the right words and conviction to dig agonizingly into the soul of southern Maryland's racial divide. I was moved by the fact that folks listened to what I had to say.

Then as a sophomore at St. Mary's College, I joined the speech team. Marian, our coach and Director of Minority Affairs, trekked us north to Bloomsburg College in Pennsylvania for the all-novice competition. I was the only student on my team to place in the finals, coming in fifth in the dramatic interpretation event. Speaking of drama, I was pissed. I told her that I did not ride five hours to do so poorly. She said I was ungrateful and should consider the feelings of my team members who earned no recognition at all. The following year, Marian left the college for another career, and I quit the team, unwilling to accept that level of humility.

During my junior year, Umar Hasan from Howard University began to volunteer at St. Mary's to help improve our ailing speech team. I rejoined, but was on the verge of kicking his Black ass every other week. To say he was tough is as if saying September 11th was not such a good day for a few people. When I stood before him giving raw, unrehearsed performances, (since I thought I was the bomb without practicing), Umar would get in my face and say, "Do you honestly expect me to cosign this bullshit?! If you don't want to work hard and do exactly what I told you, you can hit the door — and kiss my ass on the way out!" I insisted I would report him, but was too terrified to do so. He was insane.

By the next semester, I began to place first in almost every category in which I competed. By the end of my senior year, I had won almost fifty trophies and was recognized in all the regional newspapers. My family members framed the reports of my success and shared stories among their friends that made me seem as legendary as Oprah. However, the big competition had yet to come. There are two levels of national championships. For the National Forensics Association, one qualifies when he or she places in the finals in any event at any regional competition throughout the school year. The second, the American Forensics Association (AFA), is much more difficult. A student qualifies for AFA nationals if she or he places in the top three — at least three times — during regional conferences. At the end of my senior year, I went to the AFA nationals competing in six different events. I would no longer be eligible to compete after graduation so this was it. Marian had sent word through the student government office that since she was such a star in college and did not qualify for finals at AFA, I should not get my hopes up.

During the trip, Umar was disengaged. We had grown close by this time and were a part of each other's personal lives. He promised to tell me what was going on with him during our trip back to Maryland. I felt much of who I had become in terms of my discipline and my true voice was because of Umar. If something was wrong with him, nothing else mattered to me.

I made it beyond the preliminary rounds in two events, and past the quarter- and semi-finals in one other event. When I advanced to the final round in poetry interpretation, I gave it my all and was sure that my "game" was tighter than everybody else's in that room. The competition requires six judges to score the final rounds. When I noticed one judge who had consistently given me low scores prior to this competition, I knew there was no way I would win. Then I learned I had gotten 4th place at the big ceremony in front of at least one thousand people; I was back at that novice competition three years earlier, disappointed and unfulfilled. Umar taught me to believe I owned first place.

While seated next to me on the plane ride home, Umar said he had AIDS. My world was rocked, but not for the same reason as his. He had known about the infection for some time, but was devastated because Miles now knew and ended their relationship abruptly the night before our trip. Miles was a beautiful brotha from Baltimore who began freshman year with me at SMC. Umar felt that since he and Miles used condoms consistently, there was no reason to announce that he had AIDS. But while at a dance club the night before departing for nationals, Umar had lost control of his bowels. He ran all the way home from the club, leaving Miles to figure out things on his own. I felt for Miles, but could only think about how useless I would be without Umar in my world. He died a year and a half later.

Umar was an amazing person. He is one of the many positive men who came into my life and helped turn the ships around. I still believe in brothas, but I struggle daily with how to care for and support them, without losing myself in the process.

$\mathscr{N}$OBODY'S FAULT BUT MINE

Nina Simone, The Blind Boys of Alabama, The Staple Singers, and numerous other blues and gospel artists recorded a song that goes, "Nobody's fault but mine. Nobody's fault but mine. If I die and my soul be lost, it's nobody's fault but mine." I insist this song was created just for me because my wholeness has centered primarily around taking full responsibility for my emotions, my empowerment, and my joy.

I've been through a lot, but not nearly as much as many sistas who don't have the basics to work with. Relatively speaking, I've had a good life. I have attended schools where teachers care, I have always had a home in which to live, and I am physically able to work. Thus, I have never had any reason to complain about material resources. Struggle, for me, has stemmed from an attempt to negotiate my sense of self in light of contradictions embedded within my desires and intuition.

For example, I am one of the many sistas in America who have worked hard, who made education a priority, and who have acquired many accoutrements of success. In general, I have it going on. Yet, many brothas find my success intimidating when considering me for partnership. Nowhere in my education have I been taught how to be satisfied with *stuff* and without the affections of another human being. Everywhere in my social experience, I was taught to make myself smaller, to minimize, and to settle for whatever intimacy is available to me now.

I work through it, though, one day at a time.

The bottom line is I have chosen to do well in spite of the ghetto, the loss of my brother, the poor choices, the contradictions inherent in being a strong Black woman, and the letdowns. Life is, in part, about choices. But it is largely about how we deal with consequences.

Success is a process, and much of mine has come from a willingness to use words with compassion and conviction, and to speak truth fearlessly the way I see it. I do so, unabashedly, because I don't fear the consequences of being candid and painfully honest about my own life. Sometimes, however, keepin' it real with myself seems like the most difficult task in the universe. Trying to manage my ego alongside what I've been through, infused with the struggle to forgive my transgressions, has been a task I've attempted to avoid more than I care to admit. My innermost dialogue sometimes sounds like my father's voice, sometimes like the men who have seen me as unworthy, sometimes like that of Tiffany—confused and torn. It's a full time job keeping my emotions healthy.

I fall down. I get up. I fall again. Often. But I am not a victim. That's been the key.

If I die and my soul be lost, it's nobody's fault by mine. . . .

$\mathscr{E}$PILOGUE

In a couple small doses here, I mention that I have a sexual interest in women. It's critical that I note that my intimate relationships with women helped define, in large part, who I am. However, I've chosen to focus in this text on how some of my identity was shaped through my interactions with men: my father, my brother, Umar, my uncle, Nadir, etc.

In a separate forthcoming narrative, with a stronger lean toward third-wave feminism and woman-centered communities, I plan to examine the politics and dynamics of my identity as a bisexual woman. Doing so is neither an afterthought nor an indication that I lack the courage or conviction to do it now. I'm choosing to see the two projects as having separate aims and consequences, and I've made the choice to discuss the issues through a shift in focus.

Fly Free!

3842800

Made in the USA